Growing in Grace

KNOWING AND LOVING GOD THROUGH SPIRITUAL DISCIPLINES

JOANNA KIMBREL & STEFANIE BOYLES

Study Suggestions

We believe that the Bible is true, trustworthy, and timeless and that it is vitally important for all believers. These study suggestions are intended to help you more effectively study Scripture as you seek to know and love God through His Word.

SUGGESTED STUDY TOOLS

- A Bible

- A double-spaced, printed copy of the Scripture passages that this study covers. You can use a website like *www.biblegateway.com* to copy the text of a passage and print out a double-spaced copy to be able to mark on easily.

- A journal to write notes or prayers

- Pens, colored pencils, and highlighters

- A dictionary to look up unfamiliar words

HOW TO USE THIS STUDY

Begin your study time in prayer. Ask God to reveal Himself to you, to help you understand what you are reading, and to transform you with His Word (Psalm 119:18).

Before you read what is written in each day of the study itself, read the assigned passages of Scripture for that day. Use your double-spaced copy to circle, underline, highlight, draw arrows, and mark in any way you would like to help you dig deeper as you work through a passage.

Read the daily written content provided for the current study day.

Answer the questions that appear at the end of each study day.

HOW TO STUDY THE BIBLE

The inductive method provides tools for deeper and more intentional Bible study. To study a book of the Bible inductively, work through the steps below after reading background information on the book.

1. OBSERVATION & COMPREHENSION
Key question: What does the text say?

After reading the book of the Bible in its entirety at least once, begin working with smaller portions of the book. Read a passage of Scripture repetitively, and then mark the following items in the text:

- Key or repeated words and ideas
- Key themes
- Transition words (*Ex: therefore, but, because, if/then, likewise, etc.*)
- Lists
- Comparisons & Contrasts
- Commands
- Unfamiliar words (look these up in a dictionary)
- Questions you have about the text

2. INTERPRETATION
Key question: What does the text mean?

Once you have annotated the text, work through the following steps to help you interpret its meaning:

- Read the passage in other versions for a better understanding of the text.
- Read cross-references to help interpret Scripture with Scripture.
- Paraphrase or summarize the passage to check for understanding.
- Identify how the text reflects the metanarrative of Scripture, which is the story of creation, fall, redemption, and restoration.
- Read trustworthy commentaries if you need further insight into the meaning of the passage.

3 APPLICATION
Key Question: How should the truth of this passage change me?

Bible study is not merely an intellectual pursuit. The truths about God, ourselves, and the gospel that we discover in Scripture should produce transformation in our hearts and lives. Answer the following questions as you consider what you have learned in your study:

- What attributes of God's character are revealed in the passage?

    Consider places where the text directly states the character of God, as well as how His character is revealed through His words and actions.

- What do I learn about myself in light of who God is?

    Consider how you fall short of God's character, how the text reveals your sin nature, and what it says about your new identity in Christ.

- How should this truth change me?

    A passage of Scripture may contain direct commands telling us what to do or warnings about sins to avoid in order to help us grow in holiness. Other times our application flows out of seeing ourselves in light of God's character. As we pray and reflect on how God is calling us to change in light of His Word, we should be asking questions like, "How should I pray for God to change my heart?" and "What practical steps can I take toward cultivating habits of holiness?"

ATTRIBUTES OF GOD

ETERNAL
God has no beginning and no end. He always was, always is, and always will be.

HAB 1:12 / REV. 1:8 / IS. 41:4

FAITHFUL
God is incapable of anything but fidelity. He is loyally devoted to His plan and purpose.

2 TIM. 2:13 / DEUT. 7:9
HEB. 10:23

GLORIOUS
God is ultimately beautiful, deserving of all praise and honor.

REV. 19:1 / PS. 104:1
EX. 40:34-35

GOOD
God is pure; there is no defilement in Him. He is unable to sin, and all He does is good.

GEN. 1:31 / PS. 34:8 / PS. 107:1

GRACIOUS
God is kind, giving to us gifts and benefits which we do not deserve.

2 KINGS 13:23 / PS. 145:8
IS. 30:18

HOLY
God is undefiled and unable to be in the presence of defilement. He is sacred and set-apart.

REV. 4:8 / LEV. 19:2 / HAB. 1:13

IMMUTABLE
God does not change. He is the same yesterday, today, and tomorrow.

1 SAM. 15:29 / ROM. 11:29
JAMES 1:17

JEALOUS
God is desirous of receiving the praise and affection He rightly deserves.

EX. 20:5 / DEUT. 4:23-24
JOSH. 24:19

JUST
God governs in perfect justice. He acts in accordance with justice. In Him there is no wrongdoing or dishonesty.

IS. 61:8 / DEUT. 32:4 / PS. 146:7-9

LOVE
God is eternally, enduringly, steadfastly loving and affectionate. He does not forsake or betray His covenant love.

JN. 3:16 / EPH. 2:4-5 / 1 JN. 4:16

MERCIFUL
God is compassionate, withholding us from the wrath that we deserve.

TITUS 3:5 / PS. 25:10
LAM. 3:22-23

OMNIPOTENT
God is all-powerful; His strength is unlimited.

MAT. 19:26 / JOB 42:1-2
JER. 32:27

OMNIPRESENT
God is everywhere; His presence is near and permeating.

PROV. 15:3 / PS. 139:7-10
JER. 23:23-24

OMNISCIENT
God is all-knowing; there is nothing unknown to Him.

PS. 147:4 / 1 JN. 3:20
HEB. 4:13

PATIENT
God is long-suffering and enduring. He gives ample opportunity for people to turn toward Him.

ROM. 2:4 / 2 PET. 3:9 / PS. 86:15

RIGHTEOUS
God is blameless and upright. There is no wrong found in Him.

PS. 119:137 / JER. 12:1
REV. 15:3

SOVEREIGN
God governs over all things; He is in complete control.

COL. 1:17 / PS. 24:1-2
1 CHRON. 29:11-12

TRUE
God is our measurement of what is fact. By Him are we able to discern true and false.

JN. 3:33 / ROM. 1:25 / JN. 14:6

WISE
God is infinitely knowledgeable and is judicious with His knowledge.

IS. 46:9-10 / IS. 55:9 / PROV. 3:19

METANARRATIVE OF SCRIPTURE

Creation

In the beginning, God created the universe. He made the world and everything in it. He created humans in His own image to be His representatives on the earth.

Fall

The first humans, Adam and Eve, disobeyed God by eating from the fruit of the Tree of Knowledge of Good and Evil. Because of sin, the world was cursed. The punishment for sin is death, and because of Adam's original sin, all humans are sinful and condemned to death.

Redemption

God sent his Son to become a human and redeem His people. Jesus Christ lived a sinless life but died on the cross to pay the penalty for sin. He resurrected from the dead and ascended into heaven. All who put their faith in Jesus are saved from death and freely receive the gift of eternal life.

Restoration

One day, Jesus Christ will return again and restore all that sin destroyed. He will usher in a new heaven and new earth where all who trust in Him will live eternally with glorified bodies in the presence of God.

IN THIS STUDY

Week 1

WHAT ARE SPIRITUAL DISCIPLINES?   11
THE GOSPEL & SPIRITUAL DISCIPLINES   15
EVALUATING OUR TIME   19
BIBLE INTAKE   27
HEARING GOD'S WORD   31
SCRIPTURE MEMORY: 2 PET. 1:3   35
WEEKLY REFLECTION   36

Week 2

READING & STUDYING GOD'S WORD   39
READING & STUDYING GOD'S WORD TOGETHER   47
SCRIPTURE MEMORIZATION   51
MEDITATING ON GOD'S WORD   57
WORSHIP   61
SCRIPTURE MEMORY: PS. 119:103   65
WEEKLY REFLECTION   66

Week 3

PERSONAL PRAYER 69
CORPORATE PRAYER 75
FELLOWSHIP OF BELIEVERS 79
SERVING 83
EVANGELISM 87
SCRIPTURE MEMORY: EPH. 4:15-16 91
WEEKLY REFLECTION 92

Week 4

FASTING 95
SILENCE & SOLITUDE 99
STEWARDSHIP 103
GIVING THANKS & REJOICING ALWAYS 107
PERSEVERANCE 111
SCRIPTURE MEMORY: PS. 62:8 115
WEEKLY REFLECTION 116

Week 1 Day 1

"THE SOUL-SATISFYING JOY
OF A FRUITFUL LIFE COMES BY THE
HARD WORK OF FAITHFULNESS!"

WHAT ARE SPIRITUAL DISCIPLINES?

Read 1 Timothy 4:8-16

The Christian life is a joy-filled life, but it does not come without work. Consider the many metaphors in Scripture—the believer is like a farmer, working hard to sow with the goal of reaping a harvest in due time, or like a soldier, submitting to the regulations set forth by a higher authority, or even an athlete, conditioning the body to successfully run the race. Discipline, obedience, and trusting in the Lord to produce the desired effects are depicted in these metaphors, and they characterize the life of a believer. Likewise, spiritual disciplines should characterize the life of every believer. But it is not just mindless, backbreaking work. It is a means to experience amazing grace and abundant joy. The soul-satisfying joy of a fruitful life comes by the hard work of faithfulness!

Spiritual disciplines are activities that believers do. Traditionally, these activities include Bible intake (hearing, reading, studying, meditating on, and memorizing Scripture), prayer, fasting, worship, service, fellowship, solitude, and celebration. Theologians have included evangelism and discipleship, stewardship, and journaling under the umbrella of spiritual disciplines as well. The thread that unites all of these activities is the end goal. The goal of each spiritual discipline is growth in intimacy with God and growth in personal godliness, which lead to exponential growth in joy and delight. These disciplines are found in Scripture, and they are to be practiced individually and corporately for the edification of the body of Christ.

In a sense, there is a mechanical aspect to these disciplines—believers find methods of praying, studying Scripture, fasting, and more. We utilize Bible reading plans and employ the inductive method of Bible study. We strategically pray, designating different days of the week to pray over various people groups and situations. We determine the specifics of our fast like how long and from what. We serve and enjoy fellowship within the structure of the local church. However, practicing the spiritual disciplines in a way that honors God and results in true spiritual maturity goes beyond mechanics. Methodology is powerless to change the inner man. While the hope is to grow in Christlikeness, the truth remains that inner transformation is a work of God. Romans 5:17 clearly states how righteousness is a free gift that comes through Jesus Christ. It cannot be earned or achieved.

Spiritual disciplines are the outworking of a redeemed heart. Believers are declared objectively righteous once they put their faith in the person and work of Christ, but the journey of growing in righteousness has only begun. Spiritual disciplines are the means of growing in godliness with the help of the Holy Spirit in the life of a believer. They are the tools to sanctify a believer, transforming him or her from the inside out. Engaging in prayer, Bible intake, Christian fellowship, and the other disciplines are responses to the work of God's grace in our lives.

There is a beautiful dynamic at play: God works in the hearts and lives of His people, and His people respond to Him by engaging in spiritual disciplines, obeying His Word, and submitting to His lordship. These are not passive behaviors.

The believer does not live an idle life leaving all the work up to God. In fact, it is impossible to remain unmoved when the Lord works in our hearts. As a new creation, there is a new way of living. It is a life of active and continual responding to His grace. It is a life marked by rhythms of confession and gratitude. Engaging in spiritual disciplines enables us to posture ourselves in a way to receive more of Him day after day. Giving God glory by being transformed into the image of His Son is the goal of the Christian life and spiritual disciplines.

Though these disciplines require effort from the individual, they are the means to abundant joy because they are the means to foster intimacy with Christ whose presence is the fullness of joy (Psalm 16:11). They are the means to freedom because they free believers from the natural inclinations of their sinful nature, disentangle them from the sins of this world, and unite them more closely to Christ. The results of a life saturated in prayer, God's Word, fasting, serving, Christian fellowship, and worship are godliness, greater affection for Christ, and the ability to accomplish every good work prepared for us to do for the glory of God (Ephesians 2:10).

Spiritual disciplines are for all believers, no matter where we are on the trajectory toward holiness. All that is required is a deep longing to know and love God. Though the intentional effort is required, the will to discipline ourselves is rooted in our hearts having been changed by the gospel. The beauty and power of the gospel is that all of our work is sustained by the truth that Christ finished the work on our behalf. He fuels our desire and ability to work for His good pleasure (Philippians 2:13)! We do not have to rely on our willpower to grow in godliness. Instead, we rest in our union with Christ, and the beauty of the gospel compels us to live in a way that aligns with Scripture. We do not have to pull ourselves up by our bootstraps and try harder; we simply need to abide in Christ. Once we "taste and see that the Lord is good" (Psalm 34:8), we continue to feast on His Word, finding it to be true sustenance for our souls. And we do it with other believers within the context of the local church. Only then will we find that we are able to grow in spiritual maturity, living a life of worship that glorifies Him and bears good fruit.

All that is required is a deep longing to know and love God.

IN YOUR OWN WORDS, WRITE A DEFINITION FOR SPIRITUAL DISCIPLINES. WHAT IS THE PURPOSE OF SPIRITUAL DISCIPLINES IN THE LIFE OF A BELIEVER?

_____
_____
_____
_____
_____
_____
_____
_____

READ 2 CORINTHIANS 5:17. SPIRITUAL DISCIPLINES ARE THE OUTWORKINGS OF A REDEEMED HEART. HOW DOES YOUR LIFE SHOWCASE YOUR SAVING FAITH IN JESUS CHRIST?

_____
_____
_____
_____
_____
_____
_____
_____

HOW IS THE CHRISTIAN LIFE A HAPPY LIFE? HOW IS THE CHRISTIAN LIFE A HARD LIFE?

_____
_____
_____
_____
_____
_____
_____
_____

Week 1 Day 2

"THE ENTIRE LIFE OF A FOLLOWER OF CHRIST IS TETHERED TO THE GOSPEL."

THE GOSPEL AND SPIRITUAL DISCIPLINES

Read Romans 5:1-11

The entire life of a follower of Christ is tethered to the gospel. While the gospel certainly does matter for one's moment of salvation, it also extends to every single aspect of life moving forward as a new creation. At the moment of conversion, an individual is declared positionally holy before God because of Christ and His atoning work on the cross. This is called justification, and it is immediately and fully given to believers. However, this moment of justification also signifies the beginning of a journey on the path of spiritual growth. This process of growing in godliness is called sanctification, and as opposed to justification, it is progressive in nature. It is a lifelong process where a believer conforms to the image of Christ by the power of the Holy Spirit. This spiritual dynamic is a reality in the life of every believer on this side of eternity.

Our involvement in the sanctifying work in our lives is engaging in spiritual disciplines. While spiritual disciplines in and of themselves do not produce holiness in us, they position us in such a way to be transformed by God. This is why spiritual disciplines are the means of grace to make us like Christ. Consider John 17:17 where Jesus prayed on behalf of His disciples, "Sanctify them by the truth; your word is truth." Followers of Jesus are sanctified by the Word of God, which is living and active (Hebrews 4:12). Yet, believers play a part in that they read, study, memorize, and meditate on Scripture, allowing the Word to do what only it can do. We position ourselves under the authority of God's holy Word, profiting from its supernatural ability to teach, rebuke, correct, and train us in righteousness (2 Timothy 3:16).

In this way, sanctification involves our will as we act on our longing for God by engaging in the spiritual disciplines. This is how and why the gospel relates to sanctification and spiritual disciplines. An essential truth of the good news of the gospel is that people cannot earn their righteousness. The gospel reminds believers that every aspect of salvation—justification, sanctification, and glorification—is the work of God. We can only engage in the disciplines in a God-honoring way by being fully dependent on the Holy Spirit because it is the Spirit who engages the will of every believer to strive toward the things of God and away from the things of this world (Philippians 2:13). This is why the Apostle Paul says in Romans 15:16 that believers are "sanctified by the Holy Spirit." We, as followers of Christ, are empowered by the indwelling Spirit.

The gospel is central to our spiritual maturity, so every single one of us needs to preach the gospel to ourselves daily. The gospel reminds us that outward conformity in the form of moral uprightness and religious piety is not the end goal of spiritual disciplines or the Christian life. The goal is conformity to Christ for His glory. The more we grow in spiritual maturity, the more we enjoy God and glorify Him in and through our lives. We pursue holiness and strive for spiritual growth, not to earn acceptance or favor from God but as an outworking of our love and devotion to Him. Those of us who put our faith in Christ have the perfect assurance of our eternal well-being, and it is out of this assurance as children of God that we strive toward holiness through spiritual disciplines.

The gospel also protects us from pride and fear. Because spiritual disciplines are things that we actively do, both pride and fear are possibilities. We can begin to view engaging in spiritual disciplines as upholding the law, which is legalism. Legalism can cause us to take pride in success or live in fear of failure. The gospel declares that Jesus perfectly fulfilled the law and that the victory has already been won. Those united to Him share in His righteousness and victory, and He has made them "competent to be ministers of a new covenant, not of the letter, but of the Spirit. For the letter kills, but the Spirit gives life" (2 Corinthians 3:6). As the gospel keeps all things God-centered instead of centered on ourselves, we experience freedom, even in our pursuit of godliness. Thus, while preaching the gospel to ourselves is not defined as a classic spiritual discipline, it is an essential practice in the life of a believer and in the practice of spiritual disciplines.

The gospel is central to our spiritual maturity.

WHAT IS SANCTIFICATION? WHAT ROLE DO SPIRITUAL DISCIPLINES PLAY IN OUR SANCTIFICATION?

___

WHY DO WE NEED TO PREACH THE GOSPEL TO OURSELVES EVERY DAY? WHAT PITFALLS DOES THE GOSPEL SAFEGUARD US FROM REGARDING SPIRITUAL DISCIPLINES?

___

WHAT IS A MAJOR BARRIER FOR YOU WHEN IT COMES TO ENGAGING IN SPIRITUAL DISCIPLINES? HOW DOES THE GOSPEL ADDRESS THAT BARRIER IN YOUR LIFE?

___

Week 1 Day 3

PRACTICING SPIRITUAL DISCIPLINES REGULARLY TAKES PLANNING AND INTENTIONALITY.

EVALUATING OUR TIME

Spiritual disciplines are just that—disciplines—and practicing them regularly will take planning and intentionality. Today, we will take some time to evaluate our schedules, priorities, and commitments to make space for spiritual disciplines.

1. FILL IN THE CALENDAR ON PAGES 20-21 WITH THE EVENTS OF A TYPICAL WEEK. INCLUDE THINGS LIKE SLEEP, STANDING APPOINTMENTS, WORK, EXERCISE, SOCIAL EVENTS, ENTERTAINMENT, AND TIME YOU SPEND ON HOUSEHOLD RESPONSIBILITIES.

   USE THE CALENDAR ON PAGES 24-25 TO MAP OUT CHANGES YOU WOULD LIKE TO MAKE TO YOUR WEEKLY ROUTINE IN ORDER TO INCORPORATE SPIRITUAL DISCIPLINES.

2. AFTER CREATING YOUR CALENDAR, RETURN TO THIS PAGE, AND WRITE OUT YOUR RESPONSIBILITIES, OBLIGATIONS, AND COMMITMENTS IN ORDER OF HIGHEST TO LOWEST PRIORITY IN THE SPACE BELOW.

*QUESTIONS CONTINUED ON PAGE 22

USE THIS SPREAD TO MAP OUT WHAT A TYPICAL WEEK LOOKS LIKE FOR YOU RIGHT NOW.

	SUNDAY	MONDAY	TUESDAY
6:00 AM			
6:30			
7:00			
7:30			
8:00			
8:30			
9:00			
9:30			
10:00			
10:30			
11:00			
11:30			
12:00 PM			
12:30			
1:00			
1:30			
2:00			
2:30			
3:00			
3:30			
4:00			
4:30			
5:00			
5:30			
6:00			
6:30			
7:00			
7:30			
8:00			
8:30			
9:00			
9:30			
10:00			
10:30			

WEDNESDAY	THURSDAY	FRIDAY	SATURDAY

3. IS THERE ANYTHING IN YOUR SCHEDULE THAT CAN BE ELIMINATED, OUTSOURCED, OR DONE MORE EFFICIENTLY?

YES:

HERE'S THE PLAN:

THINGS THAT CANNOT BE ELIMINATED:

4. APPROXIMATELY HOW MUCH TIME DO YOU SPEND EACH DAY ON SCREENS OUTSIDE OF WORK?

HOW CAN YOU LIMIT THIS TIME?

MY SCREEN TIME GOAL:

ACTION STEPS:

5. DO YOU HAVE SPACE AVAILABLE ON SUNDAYS TO GATHER IN A LOCAL CHURCH?

IF NOT, HOW CAN YOU REARRANGE YOUR SCHEDULE TO PRIORITIZE THE LOCAL CHURCH?

6. WHAT SPIRITUAL DISCIPLINES, IF ANY, ARE YOU ALREADY PRACTICING REGULARLY?

WHAT ARE THE TOP THREE DISCIPLINES YOU WOULD LIKE TO PURSUE MORE INTENTIONALLY?

1	2	3

7. WHAT TIMES EACH DAY CAN YOU DEDICATE TO PRACTICING SPIRITUAL DISCIPLINES?

USE THIS SPREAD TO MAP OUT CHANGES YOU WOULD LIKE TO MAKE TO INCORPORATE SPIRITUAL DISCIPLINES INTO YOUR WEEK.

	SUNDAY	MONDAY	TUESDAY
6:00 AM			
6:30			
7:00			
7:30			
8:00			
8:30			
9:00			
9:30			
10:00			
10:30			
11:00			
11:30			
12:00 PM			
12:30			
1:00			
1:30			
2:00			
2:30			
3:00			
3:30			
4:00			
4:30			
5:00			
5:30			
6:00			
6:30			
7:00			
7:30			
8:00			
8:30			
9:00			
9:30			
10:00			
10:30			

WEDNESDAY	THURSDAY	FRIDAY	SATURDAY

Week 1 Day 4

"THERE IS NO SPIRITUAL
DISCIPLINE MORE PROFITABLE
THAN BIBLE INTAKE."

BIBLE INTAKE

Read Psalm 19:7-11, 2 Timothy 3:14-17, John 17:17

There is no spiritual discipline more profitable than Bible intake. It is the first and most important of the disciplines from which all the others proceed. This one discipline encompasses many practices such as hearing, reading, and memorizing Scripture. To prioritize Bible intake is not to diminish the value of the other disciplines. In fact, Bible intake enriches the other spiritual disciplines and provides instruction on how they should be employed. Prioritizing Bible intake does not inhibit the practice of other spiritual disciplines but should lead to a more robust and fruitful engagement in them all.

The Bible is of the utmost importance for every believer because the Bible is the Word of God. It is inspired, which means that although its 66 books were written by different human authors, God worked through each of them to breathe His words onto the pages of the Bible. Because of its divine authorship by the all-knowing and good God who cannot lie, the Bible is also inerrant. Inerrancy means that in its original manuscripts, the Bible is without error. It is totally true and trustworthy. In its pages, God has revealed everything we need to know in order to obtain salvation and live a life of godliness. It is sufficient, and we need not look beyond Scripture for any further revelation. Finally, the Bible is eternal. It reveals the character of God who never changes; the truth of Scripture is timeless and will endure forever. Because the Bible is inspired, inerrant, sufficient, and eternal, we should look to it as our final authority on truth. The Bible informs everything we do, say, and believe because it is the Word of God.

The Bible is not optional but is vital for the Christian life. In fact, Moses described the words of the Lord as "your life" (Deuteronomy 32:47). The Bible contains the gospel, the good news that Christ died for sinners. It is through Jesus Christ alone that we can have eternal life. Because of sin, we are dead apart from the gospel, and it is the Bible that presents that gospel to us. Every page of Scripture, from beginning to end, points to the good news of Jesus Christ. It is all about Him, and we need all of it.

In a moment God brings us from death to life through faith in Jesus Christ, but the work of the gospel does not end there. Salvation is both instantaneous and ongoing as we grow to become more and more like Jesus. This process of spiritual maturity cannot take place apart from the Word of God. Through the Bible, God has revealed Himself to us. In it we see His character proclaimed and displayed through His works. It is when we behold the glory of God that we are transformed into His image, and He has shown us His glory through His Word. We are called to be holy as God Himself is holy (Leviticus 11:44, 1 Peter 1:15), and we are sanctified by the Spirit in the enduring truth of God's Word.

In 2 Timothy 3:16-17, Paul describes Scripture as useful and profitable. It transforms us and produces fruit in our lives. It teaches us about God, ourselves, and salvation. It convicts us of our sinful ways and shows us how to live according to God's commands. Through it we receive training to grow in righteousness. It is through the Bible that God forms us into mature followers of Christ. In His Word, He gives us everything we need for every good work that He has prepared for us to do. The Bible is not meant to be something that we consult occasionally when questions arise or when life becomes difficult. It is meant to inform and transform every single part of our lives. The Bible has valuable, practical implications for our lives, but its value is not merely utilitarian. The sacred words of God are a source of great joy! They are to be desired and enjoyed because they show us the One who is supremely satisfying.

The Word of God is indispensable for our spiritual life and well-being, yet it can be our tendency to view the Bible as nonessential. How would our lives be different if we approached the Word of God as something as vital to our spiritual life as food, water, and sleep are to our physical bodies? What if instead of spiritually starving ourselves by seeking sustenance from an occasional Bible verse, recorded sermon, or faith-based book, we partook daily of the bountiful nourishment of God's Word? How much sweeter might our days be if we brought our weariness to the One who promises rest for our souls? Just like we plan our meals and schedule times to sleep and wake, Bible intake will not happen on its own. It is a discipline that we must establish and work into our days. Our very lives depend on it.

The Word of God is indispensable for our spiritual life.

READ PSALM 19:7-11 AGAIN, AND LIST ALL THE ADJECTIVES THAT DAVID USES TO DESCRIBE THE WORD OF GOD AND ALL THAT HE SAYS THE WORD OF GOD DOES.

DOES READING THE WORD OF GOD FEEL MORE LIKE A DUTY OR A DELIGHT FOR YOU RIGHT NOW?

WHAT WOULD YOUR ATTITUDE TOWARD THE WORD OF GOD BE IF IT REFLECTED THE TRUE VALUE OF SCRIPTURE? WHAT DO YOUR DAILY LIFE AND ROUTINE INDICATE ABOUT HOW YOU HAVE THOUGHT ABOUT SCRIPTURE UP UNTIL NOW?

Week 1 Day 5

"IN THE GROWTH OF ALL,
GOD IS GLORIFIED."

HEARING GOD'S WORD

Read 1 Timothy 4:13, Romans 10:17, Ephesians 4:11-16

Bible intake is a necessity for the spiritual maturity of every believer, and this broad category encompasses several specific, spiritual disciplines. One of the simplest forms of Bible intake is hearing the Word of God. We must hear the message of the gospel that is presented to us in Scripture in order to believe in Christ, and we need to hear the gospel over and over again as we grow in Christlike maturity. The primary way that we can practice this spiritual discipline is by regularly attending a local church where we sit under the faithful teaching of God's Word.

The importance of regularly hearing the Bible read and preached in a local church body should not be overlooked. We may be tempted to believe that the church is not a necessary part of our spiritual growth because we can read and study the Bible for ourselves at home, but God says otherwise. In Paul's first letter to Timothy, he urges Timothy to devote himself to teaching the Word of God and reading it publicly to those whom he leads in his local context. This exhortation takes place amidst Paul's warning about false teachers who threaten to lead people away from the truth of the gospel. Gathering together to hear Scripture read and taught was vital for uniting believers in the truth in order to help keep them from wandering into demonic lies disguised as truth.

These exhortations are just as important for the contemporary church as they were for the ancient church. Even as the false teachers in 1 Timothy 4 taught that in order to be saved, believers must abstain from certain foods or remain single, many people add to the gospel today. Whether it be adherence to a strict set of rules, membership in a specific church denomination, or loyalty to one political party or another, there are many voices that make claims about the preconditions for receiving God's saving grace. But the Lord says that only one thing is required. The way to salvation is Jesus—nothing more and nothing less. With all the competing voices seeking to add to the gospel of grace—even the voice of our own sin—it is vital that we discipline ourselves to hear the Word of God. We should heed the words of the author of Hebrews who enjoins us to make a habit of gathering as the body of Christ, "not neglecting to meet together, as some are in the habit of doing, but encouraging each other, and all the more as you see the day approaching" (Hebrews 10:25).

Being a part of a local body of believers where the Bible is faithfully preached is vital for our individual and collective spiritual maturity. God has graciously given pastors to shepherd and teach according to God's Word. Through the preaching of the Word, God equips us for good works, causes us to grow in unity with one another according to Christ's righteousness, and forms us into a people who speak the truth and are united in love. Sanctification can take place on a personal level as we engage in Bible intake on our own, but God does not call us only to individual growth. The Bible calls us members of one body, and through coming together as the people of God to hear the teaching of God's Word, we grow up together as a body. As the body matures, so too does the individual in ways he or she would not otherwise alone. In the growth of all, God is glorified.

While participation in a local church where the Word of God is read and taught is the primary way that God commands us to hear the Word, there are several other supplementary practices we may choose to employ. Some find it helpful to listen to an audio Bible during a morning commute or while going for a walk. Music that is saturated with Scripture can be a wonderful way to keep God's Word in our ears. We can even hear the Word of God as we intentionally cultivate friendships with fellow believers, speaking the truth of God's Word to one another regularly.

God tells us to hear the Word, but this command is not primarily about literal sound waves in our ears. This exhortation is a call to receive the teaching of Scripture and to live in response to its truth. This is why James 1:22 warns us to be not only a hearer of God's Word but a doer. This command is for the deaf and the hearing—a call to be transformed by the Word of God.

The way to salvation is Jesus—nothing more and nothing less.

WHAT KINDS OF THINGS DO YOU HEAR, WHETHER THAT BE THROUGH PODCASTS, BLOG POSTS, MUSIC, FRIENDSHIPS, ETC., ON A DAILY BASIS? HOW DO THOSE THINGS IMPACT THE WAY YOU LIVE?

WHY IS HEARING THE WORD OF GOD IN THE CONTEXT OF A LOCAL CHURCH BODY IMPORTANT IF WE HAVE ACCESS TO GOD'S WORD AT HOME?

ARE YOU A PART OF A LOCAL CHURCH THAT PRIORITIZES THE READING AND TEACHING OF SCRIPTURE? WHAT STEPS CAN YOU TAKE TO FIND A CHURCH OR PRIORITIZE HEARING GOD'S WORD IN THIS WAY?

WEEK 1 MEMORY VERSE

His divine power has given us everything required for life and godliness through the knowledge of him who called us by his own glory and goodness.

2 PETER 1:3

Week One Reflection

REVIEW ALL PASSAGES FROM THE WEEK

SUMMARIZE THE MAIN PRINCIPLES YOU LEARNED.

WHAT DID YOU OBSERVE ABOUT GOD'S CHARACTER?

WHAT DID YOU LEARN ABOUT THE CONDITION OF MANKIND AND ABOUT YOURSELF?

HOW WERE YOU POINTED TO THE GOSPEL?

HOW DOES THE GOSPEL ENCOURAGE AND EMPOWER YOU TO PURSUE GODLINESS, AND WHAT SPECIFIC ACTION STEPS CAN YOU TAKE TO IMPLEMENT THE SPIRITUAL DISCIPLINES COVERED THIS WEEK?

WRITE A PRAYER RESPONDING TO WHAT YOU HAVE STUDIED THIS WEEK. ADORE GOD FOR HIS CHARACTER. CONFESS THE SIN THAT HE HAS REVEALED IN YOUR OWN LIFE THIS WEEK. PRAY FOR THOSE WHO THE LORD BROUGHT TO MIND AS YOU STUDIED THIS WEEK.

Week 2 Day 1

"BELIEVERS CAN TRULY KNOW
THAT THE BIBLE IS INSPIRED BY GOD
BECAUSE IT IS SELF-AUTHENTICATING."

READING AND STUDYING GOD'S WORD

Read 2 Timothy 2:15-19, 2 Timothy 3:16-17

The Bible is not an ordinary book. It was written over a span of 1,500 years by more than forty authors on three different continents in a variety of literary styles. Yet, it tells one cohesive story of God redeeming His people. This miracle is only possible due to God's incredible sovereignty. Because each human author was inspired by the Holy Spirit, there are no internal contradictions. The authenticity and reliability of the Old and New Testaments are supported by more early manuscripts than any other ancient document.

While these claims are noteworthy, believers can truly know that the Bible is inspired by God because it is self-authenticating. We know the Bible is the inspired Word of God; in His grace, He enables us to see His glory in its pages (2 Corinthians 4:4-6). The Holy Spirit bears witness in our hearts of the truth that "all Scripture is inspired by God" (2 Timothy 3:16). When we read and study His Word, we experience these truths when we are convicted, comforted, and encouraged by the living words.

It is absolutely necessary for every believer to read and study God's Word. Jesus said in Matthew 4:4, "Man must not live on bread alone but on every word that comes from the mouth of God." Akin to the nourishment that the physical body receives from food, feasting on the Word is a spiritual discipline that is vital to the overall health of the believer because the Bible is sustenance to the soul. We need every word. Because the Bible tells one, unified narrative, every book is part of the story and wisely included by God for life and godliness of His people.

Yet, it requires hard work for anyone to read and study God's Word. It requires reordering priorities in order to have the time and space to consume His living words. Believers, like anyone else, need to fight against laziness and commit to engaging their minds and hearts. Discipline is required to act on the longing we feel for God. We need to respond to the Spirit's leading and position ourselves to be sanctified by the Word of God by reading and studying it faithfully. We come in humility, seeking to know God as He reveals Himself in His Word, and we are transformed from the inside out, bit by bit.

We need to read the whole Bible. Reading the whole Bible allows us to grasp the breadth of Scripture. Having a comprehensive understanding of the overall story of Scripture allows us to be familiar with the broader themes woven throughout the Bible. Keeping the wider context in mind is helpful when diving into small portions of the Bible and understanding how a specific passage fits in the overall narrative. Reading for breadth also aids in interpretation. A helpful principle for interpreting Scripture is to allow Scripture to interpret Scripture. This principle means that the interpretation of one passage will never contradict the meaning of another passage of Scripture. There is perfect harmony throughout, and having familiarity with the whole Bible safeguards us from misinterpretation. This is why every single one of us would benefit from having a systematic plan to regularly read through the Bible in its entirety.

Studying Scripture is a separate discipline in that it involves digging into God's Word for depth. God's Word is an endless treasure trove of life-giving truths. It would take more than a lifetime to explore its depths. Bible study can look different for different people. However, the heart of Bible study is to carefully read passages of Scripture with the goal of comprehension and accurate interpretation prior to personal life application. This can be through the aid of an additional biblical resource like a Bible study book, or it can simply involve paper and pen, providing room to pour over cross-references, concordances, and other related passages of Scripture. The discipline of Bible study means slowing down and understanding the historical and cultural context of the passage, possibly through word studies and considering the original language of the text, and consulting commentaries to answer lingering questions. While Bible study can be done in a group setting, the primary legwork should be done by each believer individually.

It is profitable to read and study Scripture, and all of Scripture is necessary for us to be equipped for every good work the Lord has prepared for us (2 Timothy 3:16-17). God calls each of us to know Him, enjoy Him, and put His glory on display, and such a command requires the transformation of our minds and hearts by the power of His Word and His Spirit in us. So may we go to God's Word daily, seeking to know Him more and more as He reveals Himself in Scripture. May feasting on God's Word—reading and studying for breadth and depth—be a lifelong pursuit until we see Jesus, who is the Word, face to face.

The Bible is not an ordinary book.

WHAT WOULD YOU SAY IF SOMEONE WERE TO ASK YOU, "HOW DO YOU KNOW THE BIBLE IS TRUSTWORTHY?"

_____
_____
_____
_____
_____

WHAT IS THE DIFFERENCE BETWEEN READING THE BIBLE AND STUDYING THE BIBLE? HOW DO THESE SEPARATE DISCIPLINES PLAY OUT IN YOUR OWN LIFE?

_____
_____
_____
_____
_____
_____

WHY IS IT IMPORTANT FOR EVERY BELIEVER TO READ AND STUDY SCRIPTURE? WHAT ARE SOME SCRIPTURE REFERENCES YOU CAN COMMIT TO MEMORY TO REMIND YOU OF ITS IMPORTANCE?

_____
_____
_____
_____
_____
_____
_____

TO GET STARTED IN STUDYING THE WORD EFFECTIVELY, CHECK OUT "HOW TO STUDY THE BIBLE" ON PAGE 4 OF THIS STUDY.

USE THE BIBLE READING PLAN PROVIDED ON THE NEXT TWO PAGES TO READ THROUGH THE ENTIRE BIBLE IN ONE YEAR!

Jan

1. Gen. 1-3 ☐
2. Gen. 4-6 ☐
3. Gen. 7-9 ☐
4. Gen. 10-12 ☐
5. Gen. 13-15 ☐
6. Gen. 16-18 ☐
7. Gen. 19-21 ☐
8. Gen. 22-24 ☐
9. Gen. 25-27 ☐
10. Gen. 28-30 ☐
11. Gen. 31-33 ☐
12. Gen. 34-36 ☐
13. Gen. 37-39 ☐
14. Gen. 40-42 ☐
15. Gen. 43-46 ☐
16. Gen. 47-50 ☐
17. Exod. 1-3 ☐
18. Exod. 4-6 ☐
19. Exod. 7-9 ☐
20. Exod. 10-12 ☐
21. Exod. 13-15 ☐
22. Exod. 16-18 ☐
23. Exod. 19-21 ☐
24. Exod. 22-24 ☐
25. Exod. 25-27 ☐
26. Exod. 28-30 ☐
27. Exod. 31-33 ☐
28. Exod. 34-36 ☐
29. Exod. 37-40 ☐
30. Lev. 1-3 ☐
31. Lev. 4-6 ☐

Feb

1. Lev. 7-9 ☐
2. Lev. 10-12 ☐
3. Lev. 13-15 ☐
4. Lev. 16-18 ☐
5. Lev. 19-21 ☐
6. Lev. 22-24 ☐
7. Lev. 25-27 ☐
8. Num. 1-3 ☐
9. Num. 4-6 ☐
10. Num. 7-9 ☐
11. Num. 10-12 ☐
12. Num. 13-15 ☐
13. Num. 16-18 ☐
14. Num. 19-21 ☐
15. Num. 22-24 ☐
16. Num. 25-27 ☐
17. Num. 28-30 ☐
18. Num. 31-33 ☐
19. Num. 34-36 ☐
20. Deut. 1-3 ☐
21. Deut. 4-6 ☐
22. Deut. 7-9 ☐
23. Deut. 10-12 ☐
24. Deut. 13-15 ☐
25. Deut. 16-18 ☐
26. Deut. 19-21 ☐
27. Deut. 22-24 ☐
28. Deut. 25-27 ☐

Mar

1. Deut. 28-30 ☐
2. Deut. 31-34 ☐
3. Josh. 1-3 ☐
4. Josh. 4-6 ☐
5. Josh. 7-9 ☐
6. Josh. 10-12 ☐
7. Josh. 13-15 ☐
8. Josh. 16-18 ☐
9. Josh. 19-21 ☐
10. Josh. 22-24 ☐
11. Judg. 1-3 ☐
12. Judg. 4-6 ☐
13. Judg. 7-9 ☐
14. Judg. 10-12 ☐
15. Judg. 13-15 ☐
16. Judg. 16-18 ☐
17. Judg. 19-21 ☐
18. Ruth ☐
19. 1 Sam. 1-3 ☐
20. 1 Sam. 4-6 ☐
21. 1 Sam. 7-9 ☐
22. 1 Sam. 10-12 ☐
23. 1 Sam. 13-15 ☐
24. 1 Sam. 16-18 ☐
25. 1 Sam. 19-21 ☐
26. 1 Sam. 22-24 ☐
27. 1 Sam. 25-27 ☐
28. 1 Sam. 28-31 ☐
29. 2 Sam. 1-3 ☐
30. 2 Sam. 4-6 ☐
31. 2 Sam. 7-9 ☐

Apr

1. 2 Sam. 10-12 ☐
2. 2 Sam. 13-15 ☐
3. 2 Sam. 16-18 ☐
4. 2 Sam. 19-21 ☐
5. 2 Sam. 22-24 ☐
6. 1 King. 1-3 ☐
7. 1 King. 4-6 ☐
8. 1 King. 7-9 ☐
9. 1 King. 10-12 ☐
10. 1 King. 13-15 ☐
11. 1 King. 16-18 ☐
12. 1 King. 19-22 ☐
13. 2 King. 1-3 ☐
14. 2 King. 4-6 ☐
15. 2 King. 7-9 ☐
16. 2 King. 10-12 ☐
17. 2 King. 13-15 ☐
18. 2 King. 16-18 ☐
19. 2 King. 19-21 ☐
20. 2 King. 22-25 ☐
21. 1 Chr. 1-6 ☐
22. 1 Chr. 7-9 ☐
23. 1 Chr. 10-12 ☐
24. 1 Chr. 13-15 ☐
25. 1 Chr. 16-18 ☐
26. 1 Chr. 19-21 ☐
27. 1 Chr. 22-25 ☐
28. 1 Chr. 26-29 ☐
29. 2 Chr. 1-3 ☐
30. 2 Chr. 4-6 ☐

May

1. 2 Chr. 7-9 ☐
2. 2 Chr. 10-12 ☐
3. 2 Chr. 13-15 ☐
4. 2 Chr. 16-18 ☐
5. 2 Chr. 19-21 ☐
6. 2 Chr. 22-24 ☐
7. 2 Chr. 25-27 ☐
8. 2 Chr. 28-30 ☐
9. 2 Chr. 31-33 ☐
10. 2 Chr. 34-36 ☐
11. Ezra 1-3 ☐
12. Ezra 4-6 ☐
13. Ezra 7-10 ☐
14. Neh. 1-3 ☐
15. Neh. 4-6 ☐
16. Neh. 7-9 ☐
17. Neh. 10-13 ☐
18. Est. 1-3 ☐
19. Est. 4-6 ☐
20. Est. 7-10 ☐
21. Job 1-3 ☐
22. Job 4-6 ☐
23. Job 7-9 ☐
24. Job 10-12 ☐
25. Job 13-15 ☐
26. Job 16-18 ☐
27. Job 19-21 ☐
28. Job 22-24 ☐
29. Job 25-27 ☐
30. Job 28-30 ☐
31. Job 31-33 ☐

Jun

1. Job 34-36 ☐
2. Job 37-39 ☐
3. Job 40-42 ☐
4. Ps. 1-5 ☐
5. Ps. 6-10 ☐
6. Ps. 11-15 ☐
7. Ps. 16-20 ☐
8. Ps. 21-25 ☐
9. Ps. 26-30 ☐
10. Ps. 31-35 ☐
11. Ps. 36-40 ☐
12. Ps. 41-45 ☐
13. Ps. 46-50 ☐
14. Ps. 51-55 ☐
15. Ps. 56-60 ☐
16. Ps. 61-65 ☐
17. Ps. 66-70 ☐
18. Ps. 71-75 ☐
19. Ps. 76-80 ☐
20. Ps. 81-85 ☐
21. Ps. 86-90 ☐
22. Ps. 91-95 ☐
23. Ps. 96-100 ☐
24. Ps. 101-105 ☐
25. Ps. 106-110 ☐
26. Ps. 111-115 ☐
27. Ps. 116-120 ☐
28. Ps. 121-125 ☐
29. Ps. 126-130 ☐
30. Ps. 131-135 ☐

Jul

1. Ps. 136-140 ☐
2. Ps. 141-145 ☐
3. Ps. 146-150 ☐
4. Prov. 1-3 ☐
5. Prov. 4-6 ☐
6. Prov. 7-9 ☐
7. Prov. 10-12 ☐
8. Prov. 13-15 ☐
9. Prov. 16-18 ☐
10. Prov. 19-21 ☐
11. Prov. 22-24 ☐
12. Prov. 25-27 ☐
13. Prov. 28-31 ☐
14. Eccl. 1-3 ☐
15. Eccl. 4-6 ☐
16. Eccl. 7-9 ☐
17. Eccl. 10-12 ☐
18. S. of Sol. 1-4 ☐
19. S. of Sol. 5-8 ☐
20. Is. 1-3 ☐
21. Is. 4-6 ☐
22. Is. 7-9 ☐
23. Is. 10-12 ☐
24. Is. 13-15 ☐
25. Is. 16-18 ☐
26. Is. 19-21 ☐
27. Is. 22-24 ☐
28. Is. 25-27 ☐
29. Is. 28-30 ☐
30. Is. 31-33 ☐
31. Is. 34-36 ☐

Aug

1. Is. 37-39 ☐
2. Is. 40-42 ☐
3. Is. 43-45 ☐
4. Is. 46-48 ☐
5. Is. 49-51 ☐
6. Is. 52-54 ☐
7. Is. 55-57 ☐
8. Is. 58-60 ☐
9. Is. 61-63 ☐
10. Is. 64-66 ☐
11. Jer. 1-3 ☐
12. Jer. 4-6 ☐
13. Jer. 7-9 ☐
14. Jer. 10-12 ☐
15. Jer. 13-15 ☐
16. Jer. 16-18 ☐
17. Jer. 19-21 ☐
18. Jer. 22-24 ☐
19. Jer. 25-27 ☐
20. Jer. 28-30 ☐
21. Jer. 31-33 ☐
22. Jer. 34-36 ☐
23. Jer. 37-39 ☐
24. Jer. 40-42 ☐
25. Jer. 43-45 ☐
26. Jer. 46-48 ☐
27. Jer. 49-52 ☐
28. Lam. 1-3 ☐
29. Lam. 4-5 ☐
30. Ezek. 1-3 ☐
31. Ezek. 4-6 ☐

Sep

1. Ezek. 7-9 ☐
2. Ezek. 10-12 ☐
3. Ezek. 13-15 ☐
4. Ezek. 16-18 ☐
5. Ezek. 19-21 ☐
6. Ezek. 22-24 ☐
7. Ezek. 25-27 ☐
8. Ezek. 28-30 ☐
9. Ezek. 31-33 ☐
10. Ezek. 34-36 ☐
11. Ezek. 37-40 ☐
12. Ezek. 41-44 ☐
13. Ezek. 45-48 ☐
14. Dan. 1-3 ☐
15. Dan. 4-6 ☐
16. Dan. 7-9 ☐
17. Dan. 10-12 ☐
18. Hos. 1-3 ☐
19. Hos. 4-6 ☐
20. Hos. 7-10 ☐
21. Hos. 11-14 ☐
22. Joel ☐
23. Amos 1-3 ☐
24. Amos 4-6 ☐
25. Amos 7-9 ☐
26. Obadiah ☐
27. Jonah ☐
28. Micah 1-3 ☐
29. Micah 4-7 ☐
30. Nahum ☐

Oct

1. Habakkuk ☐
2. Zephaniah ☐
3. Haggai ☐
4. Zech. 1-3 ☐
5. Zech. 4-6 ☐
6. Zech. 7-10 ☐
7. Zech. 11-14 ☐
8. Mal. 1-2 ☐
9. Mal. 3-4 ☐
10. Mat. 1-3 ☐
11. Mat. 4-6 ☐
12. Mat. 7-9 ☐
13. Mat. 10-12 ☐
14. Mat. 13-15 ☐
15. Mat. 16-18 ☐
16. Mat. 19-21 ☐
17. Mat. 22-24 ☐
18. Mat. 25-28 ☐
19. Mark 1-3 ☐
20. Mark 4-6 ☐
21. Mark 7-9 ☐
22. Mark 10-12 ☐
23. Mark 13-16 ☐
24. Luke 1-3 ☐
25. Luke 4-6 ☐
26. Luke 7-9 ☐
27. Luke 10-12 ☐
28. Luke 13-15 ☐
29. Luke 16-18 ☐
30. Luke 19-21 ☐
31. Luke 22-24 ☐

Nov

1. John 1-3 ☐
2. John 4-6 ☐
3. John 7-9 ☐
4. John 10-12 ☐
5. John 13-15 ☐
6. John 16-18 ☐
7. John 19-21 ☐
8. Acts 1-3 ☐
9. Acts 4-6 ☐
10. Acts 7-9 ☐
11. Acts 10-12 ☐
12. Acts 13-15 ☐
13. Acts 16-18 ☐
14. Acts 19-21 ☐
15. Acts 22-24 ☐
16. Acts 25-28 ☐
17. Rom. 1-3 ☐
18. Rom. 4-6 ☐
19. Rom. 7-9 ☐
20. Rom. 10-12 ☐
21. Rom. 13-16 ☐
22. 1 Cor. 1-3 ☐
23. 1 Cor. 4-6 ☐
24. 1 Cor. 7-9 ☐
25. 1 Cor. 10-12 ☐
26. 1 Cor. 13-16 ☐
27. 2 Cor. 1-3 ☐
28. 2 Cor. 4-6 ☐
29. 2 Cor. 7-9 ☐
30. 2 Cor. 10-13 ☐

Dec

1. Gal. 1-3 ☐
2. Gal. 4-6 ☐
3. Eph. 1-3 ☐
4. Eph. 4-6 ☐
5. Philippians ☐
6. Colossians ☐
7. 1 Thess. ☐
8. 2 Thess. ☐
9. 1 Tim. 1-3 ☐
10. 1 Tim. 4-6 ☐
11. 2 Timothy ☐
12. Titus ☐
13. Philemon ☐
14. Heb. 1-3 ☐
15. Heb. 4-6 ☐
16. Heb. 7-9 ☐
17. Heb. 10-13 ☐
18. James 1-3 ☐
19. James 4-5 ☐
20. 1 Peter ☐
21. 2 Peter ☐
22. 1 John 1-3 ☐
23. 1 John 4-5 ☐
24. 2 John–Jude ☐
25. Rev. 1-3 ☐
26. Rev. 4-6 ☐
27. Rev. 7-9 ☐
28. Rev. 10-12 ☐
29. Rev. 13-15 ☐
30. Rev. 16-19 ☐
31. Rev. 20-22 ☐

USE THIS SPACE TO MAKE A LIST OF BIBLE STUDY GOALS AND IDEAS.

Week 5 Day 2

"STUDYING SCRIPTURE TOGETHER HELPS US TO DEEPEN OUR KNOWLEDGE OF GOD, OF OURSELVES, AND OF OTHERS."

READING AND STUDYING GOD'S WORD TOGETHER

Read 1 Corinthians 12:12-26, Proverbs 27:17, Ecclesiastes 4:9

It is vital for the believer's sanctification to learn to read, understand, interpret, and apply the Bible on his or her own, but studying Scripture with others also produces important spiritual fruit. Studying Scripture in community can take many forms, from working through a book of the Bible at a coffee shop with one other person, to a group Bible study at a local church, but they are all valuable for our spiritual maturity. Studying Scripture together helps us to deepen our knowledge of God, of ourselves, and of others.

The practice of studying the Word of God with others is rooted in God's design for believers. We are not meant to live life alone but rather, together as a whole. Scripture repeatedly uses the metaphor of a body to describe Christians. Each believer is a member of the body, and all of the individual parts work together in their various capacities to form a healthy, well-functioning body. Each member of the body has God-given gifts that are given for the good of the body, and just as a liver has a different function than the lungs, these gifts differ from one believer to another. We benefit from the gifts of other believers, and our gifts are intended for their good. This principle also applies to the study of Scripture. We are better together.

When we study Scripture together, our knowledge of God is deepened. In individual study, it is common to recognize the same attributes of God based on what God has been teaching us or on our own personal experience. While one person may quickly recognize God's power and might in Scripture, someone else might more easily pick up on His mercy and grace. When we study Scripture together, we learn to recognize themes that we might otherwise overlook, and our new insight, in turn, makes its way into our personal study. The more we study Scripture together, the fuller our vision of who God has revealed Himself to be in the Bible.

Studying Scripture alongside others also helps us to learn more about ourselves. In one sense, this self-knowledge flows directly out of the fuller knowledge of God that stems from studying the Bible with others. A glimpse of His grandness makes us keenly aware of how small we are. In seeing His strength, we see our weakness. Knowing that He needs nothing or no one reveals our great need for Him. Our knowledge of self is also deepened as others highlight passages that we might naturally rush through on our own. Acknowledging our faults can be uncomfortable, and we may move quickly through parts of the Bible that confront our own sin issues when we are studying on our own. When we study Scripture with others, we are forced to face these uncomfortable passages. This discomfort is a good thing because it makes way for confession. 1 John 1:9 assures us that confession brings about forgiveness and cleansing, and so it is a gift of God's grace when our fellow believers can call us to repentance. Sharing our sin struggles with others in this context also gives opportunity for others to pray for us, hold us accountable, and support us as we battle sin and walk in obedience.

Studying Scripture together encourages looking upward to God and inward to our own hearts, but it also facilitates looking outward. When we study Scripture with others, we have the opportunity to see how God's Word applies to people with different circumstances, backgrounds, and sin patterns. It may be easy to apply God's Word to our particular life seasons and struggles, but as we study God's Word together, we have the blessing of seeing how the truth of the gospel brings hope to all kinds of situations. When we come together around God's Word and hear the message of the gospel from the mouths of those who have experienced different hardships and struggles than us, we begin to see real people behind the sins that we have not personally experienced. In place of pride and judgment, by God's grace, our hearts are moved toward empathy and love. Studying God's Word together strengthens our ability to minister to others who are different from us.

Studying Scripture with others can increase our love and knowledge of God, lead us to repentance, and help us to love our neighbors. As we study together, we are sanctified and unified as the body of Christ. Making time to study together is not always convenient, and we may fear judgment or vulnerability, but it is worth it. God has given us one another for our encouragement, growth, and for His glory.

When we study Scripture together, our knowledge of God is deepened.

WHAT ARE SOME THINGS THAT MIGHT KEEP YOU FROM STUDYING SCRIPTURE WITH OTHERS?

WHAT PARTS OF THE BIBLE DO YOU GRAVITATE TOWARD? WHAT PARTS DO YOU TEND TO SKIP OVER? GIVEN THESE TENDENCIES, HOW MIGHT STUDYING SCRIPTURE WITH OTHERS HELP YOUR SPIRITUAL GROWTH?

READ MATTHEW 22:36-39. HOW CAN STUDYING SCRIPTURE WITH OTHERS HELP YOU FOLLOW THESE COMMANDMENTS?

Week 2 Day 3

"SCRIPTURE MEMORIZATION IS THE DISCIPLINE THAT ALLOWS FOR A DEEP, TRANSFORMING CONNECTION BETWEEN THE WORD OF GOD AND THE HEART AND MIND OF MAN."

SCRIPTURE MEMORIZATION

Read Psalm 19:7-14, Psalm 119:1-16

When it comes to putting in the effort to commit something to memory, we know it will only happen if it is something we personally deem as important. We memorize social security numbers and our significant others' phone numbers. We memorize our children's birthdays and debit card pin numbers. This information is valuable to us, so we do whatever we need to keep it stored in our memory banks. So when it comes to Scripture memorization, we have to ask ourselves if we value God's Word as important and of superior value.

The law of God elicits different reactions from believers. Some hold tightly to a banner of grace, completely abandoning the law, while others glorify the law and miss the reality of His grace. However, the law of God is a gift of grace, and it is given for the good of His people. Even in the New Testament, Jesus, who perfectly fulfilled the law, said, "whoever does and teaches these commands will be called great in the kingdom of heaven" (Matthew 5:19). The Apostle Paul notes in Acts 7:38 that Moses "received living oracles to give to us." These living words of God were to be on the hearts of God's people, ever on their lips, and they were to diligently pass them down to future generations (Deuteronomy 6:4-9). The words in Scripture are not mere words. As David said, God's Word renews our lives, makes us wise, is right and makes our hearts glad, makes our eyes light up, and is more desirable than gold. There is great reward for those who live according to its instruction!

Throughout the Old and New Testament, it is evident that those who understood God's grace also deeply loved God's law. This is true for God's people today as well. The likelihood of a believer committing Scripture to memory is slim if there is not a proper understanding and reverence for the commandments and precepts of God found in His Word. Memorization requires brainpower. A complex web of synaptic connections are made throughout the brain and reactivated as memorized information is called to mind. These connections are made by frequent exposure. God, in His infinite wisdom, created His image-bearers with brains that have the ability to do this, and it is a gift. It offers the means to formulate a deep connection between God's Word and our hearts and minds. But in order to develop the spiritual discipline of Scripture memorization, we need to see the glory of Christ in the Word of God, long to be conformed to the image of Christ, and have the discipline to repeatedly subject ourselves to the words in order to commit them to memory.

Scripture memorization is the discipline that allows for a deep, transforming connection between the Word of God and the heart and mind of man. Committing Bible verses to memory provides the means for us to obey the instruction, "Let the word of Christ dwell richly among [us]" (Colossians 3:16), meditate on the Lord's instructions day and night (Psalm 1:2), and treasure His Word in our hearts so that we may not sin against God (Psalm 119:11). When we memorize Scripture, we are exposing ourselves to biblical truths that the Holy Spirit uses to transform us from the inside out. Memorizing Scripture is a powerful way to deeply gaze at the glory of Christ and be in a position for the Word's power to change and mold our hearts and minds at any time.

Scripture memory is also necessary for us to live on this side of heaven where "the whole world is under the sway of the evil one" (1 John 5:19). Believers are to live every day dressed in the armor of God in order to effectively stand against the rulers, authorities, cosmic powers of darkness, and evil, spiritual forces (Ephesians 6:10-20). The only offensive weapon in the armor of God is the sword of the Spirit, which is the Word of God. Only the Word of God has the ability to victoriously fight against the devil. Wielding the sword of the Spirit at all times is only possible through Scripture memorization, and this continual readiness is necessary to successfully overcome the temptation to sin and not buy into lies.

Scripture memory also provides internal fortitude. As we rehearse the promises of God and familiarize ourselves with the warnings of God in the process of memorization, we are building a security system to detect errors. God's Word is protective and prescriptive for how we can best live to the glory of God. It is not burdensome or restrictive. This spiritual discipline leads to fruitful, spiritual formation. Scripture memory will enrich our prayer lives. It will equip us to minister to those in need because His words have power. It will sharpen our ability to engage in evangelism and discipleship. It will inform our worldview, conforming both heart and mind to see all things from God's viewpoint. It will allow for Scripture meditation, which leads to a deeper understanding of God's Word and appropriate application to life. It is a discipline worth intentional time and effort.

There are many systems to aid in the memorization of Scripture, but every single one of them shares one facet—repetition. Repetition is the way human brains establish enduring connections for future recollection. It is incredibly helpful for us to memorize what we are currently studying because understanding the context and meaning of the passage will bring purpose to the memorization. But we have to remember that rote memorization is not the goal. Retention is not the goal. The goal is to know God more by internalizing the truths of God's Word in our souls as His words move from our heads to our hearts and overflow into the way we live.

God's Word renews our lives.

REREAD PSALM 19:7-8, 10-11. DO YOU SHARE THESE SENTIMENTS ABOUT SCRIPTURE? HOW DO YOU FEEL ABOUT GOD'S LAW? DO YOU LOVE IT OR WRESTLE WITH ITS RELEVANCE TODAY?

___

WHAT ARE THE GOALS IN MEMORIZING SCRIPTURE? WHY IS SCRIPTURE MEMORIZATION A WORTHWHILE ENDEAVOR?

___

WHAT BENEFIT IS THERE TO MEMORIZE SCRIPTURE WHEN THE BIBLE SEEMS TO BE READILY AVAILABLE IN MOST COUNTRIES?

___

Practical Tips for Scripture Memorization

There are many systems to aid in the memorization of Scripture, but every single one of them shares one facet—repetition. No matter what verse or extended passage you want to commit to memory, you must rehearse it repeatedly. Here are some practical tips to help you navigate picking a verse or passage to memorize and how to actually commit it to memory!

HOW TO PICK A VERSE OR PASSAGE TO MEMORIZE:

- Pick a verse or passage that you are currently studying.
- If you are not doing a deep dive into a specific book or passage, you can use a topical system. Just keep in mind the context of the verse to guard against improper interpretation and application.
- There are many foundational verses of the Christian faith that are helpful for all believers to know (see options below).

TIP AND TRICKS TO COMMITTING A VERSE OR PASSAGE TO MEMORY:

- Engage all of your senses:
  - Read the verse or passage repetitively.
  - Listen to the verse or passage repetitively.
  - Write it down.
  - Say it out loud.
- Get accountability. Find a friend, and check in with each other weekly.
- Use the first letter method. Write down the first letter of each word on your hand to serve as memory prompts.
- Write the verse on index cards to post in places around your house like in front of the sink, on your bathroom mirror, by the garbage can, on the pantry door, or even on your shower wall (but be sure to put it in a plastic bag first!).
- Have anchors in your day when you rehearse it. You could recite it in the carpool line, at red lights, during your workout, while you do dishes, or while you fold laundry. It is easier to develop habits when you tether the verse to already established anchors in your daily routine.

OTHER HELPFUL RESOURCES:

- Ep. 63 *How and Why to Memorize Scripture* by Daily Grace (podcast)
- *Dwell Scripture Memory Journal* from The Daily Grace Co.
- *Scripture Memory Journal* from The Daily Grace Co.
- Verse Cards by The Daily Grace Co. (a variety of topics are available)
- Navigators Topical Memory System *(www.navigators.org)*
- Desiring God's Fighter Verses *(www.fighterverses.com)*
- *An Approach to Extended Memorization of Scripture* by Andrew M. Davis
- Bible Memory App.

USE THIS SPACE TO MAKE A LIST OF SCRIPTURE MEMORY GOALS AND IDEAS.

Week 2 Day 4

"BIBLICAL MEDITATION IS NOT EMPTYING THE MIND BUT FILLING IT WITH GOD'S WORD."

MEDITATING ON GOD'S WORD

Read Joshua 1:7-9, Psalm 63:5-6, Philippians 4:8

We can spend our days filling our minds with Scripture, but it would all be for nothing if our hearts are not changed by its truth. The Holy Spirit is the one who works transformation in us through the Word of God, and we are called to join the Spirit in the sanctification process. One of the means through which God causes His Word to move from the head to the heart is the discipline of meditation.

The word "meditation" might bring to mind mantras or mindfulness, but biblical meditation looks different than other forms of meditation. It means to think deeply. It has the sense of pondering or intently concentrating on something. In some forms of meditation, the object of meditation is a sound, a mantra, or an object with a goal being to empty the mind of all else. Biblical meditation is not emptying the mind but filling it with God's Word. While eastern meditation is inwardly focused, Biblical meditation focuses on God. Some forms of meditation seek to cease thinking, but the methodology of Biblical meditation is to ponder the glorious truths of God that He has revealed to us in Scripture.

The goal of meditating on God's Word is to be transformed by the truth of His Word. Reading, hearing, studying, and memorizing Scripture are all extremely helpful, but it is possible to go through the motions of these disciplines and fail to go beyond the intellectual. Scripture meditation is a means to move from knowledge to application. Consider Moses' words to Joshua as he prepared to lead the Israelites into the Promised Land. He told him to meditate on the Word of God but not as an end in itself. The command to meditate was so that he could be careful to do all that is written in the book of the Law. The purpose of the command to meditate was to produce obedience to the Word of God. Through the practice of meditation on the Bible, we can obey the command to be not only those who hear God's Word but those who do it (James 1:22).

Lest we think the goal of obedience to God's Word is an unmotivating reason to practice biblical meditation, the Bible's exhortations to meditate are rooted in the promise of blessing and joy. The psalmist described his response to meditating on God's Word with language of feasting and rejoicing. When he pondered the Lord—His character and His works—the result was satisfaction and delight. It can be easy to become discouraged in studying the Bible because it can sometimes feel dry. We can become disheartened if the Word of God does not captivate us or if we lose the passion for reading the Bible. While our emotional response is not the measure of the impact of God's Word on our lives, and much of our spiritual growth is unaccompanied by dramatic emotional responses, we should not let that be an excuse to remain unchanged and simply read Scripture with our heads but never our hearts. As we meditate on the Word of God, thinking deeply on gospel truths and on the works and character of God revealed in Scripture, our hearts grow to rejoice in His Word. As we behold the glory of God in His Word, His beauty changes us, and it becomes a joy to walk in His ways.

There are many ways to practice biblical meditation. We can meditate on a verse, a word or theme in a verse, or a particular concept found in a passage. While our Bible study will often cover large portions of Scripture, it is best to focus our meditation on something smaller and more specific. Scripture meditation works best when it accompanies normal Bible study. When we choose a verse, theme, or concept from a passage of Scripture that we are already studying, we will have a better understanding of the meaning of the verse and its context. In order to meditate on a verse, it is helpful to read it repeatedly or journal about its implications. Engaging creatively through painting, art journaling, or some other medium can be a helpful way to ponder the passage. Having a physical reminder like a verse card to carry around throughout the day can be a helpful way as well to meditate on Scripture. Whatever method we choose, the goal is to think deeply about the truths found in Scripture. When we set our minds on the Word of God, our hearts and lives will be changed.

Scripture meditation is a means to move from knowledge to application.

READ PSALM 1. ACCORDING TO THIS PASSAGE, WHAT FRUIT CAN MEDITATION PRODUCE IN THE LIFE OF A BELIEVER?

CHOOSE ONE OF THE VERSES FROM TODAY'S READINGS TO MEDITATE ON. USE THE SPACE BELOW TO WRITE ABOUT THE VERSE, WHAT IT REVEALS ABOUT GOD, AND ITS IMPLICATIONS FOR YOUR LIFE.

WHAT ARE SOME WAYS YOU CAN INTENTIONALLY MEDITATE ON THIS VERSE THROUGHOUT THE REST OF THE DAY?

Week 2 Day 5

"IN ORDER FOR WORSHIP TO BE SINCERE, IT MUST HAVE AN INTERNAL COMPONENT."

WORSHIP

Read John 4:21-24, Romans 12:1-2, Hebrews 10:24-25

Worship is a spiritual discipline that is frequently misunderstood. While many equate worship with singing songs about God, worship is so much more than a twenty-minute portion of a church service. To worship God is to glorify Him. It is to ascribe to the Lord the glory, worth, honor, and praise that He is due. The Greek and Hebrew words that translate to worship in the Bible carry the sense of bowing down, kneeling, or serving. Worship, then, is serving and honoring God in love and humility. It is the means by which we can fulfill our ultimate purpose as stated in the Westminster Confession: "To glorify God and enjoy Him forever."

Worship is not simply proclaiming or singing about who God is, although that is certainly an important part of worship. In order for worship to be sincere, it must have an internal component. In an encounter with a Samaritan woman, Jesus explained that true worshipers will worship both in spirit and in truth. Worshiping in spirit implies that worship is not simply an outward activity but is a matter of the heart. Genuine worship flows out of amazement and love for who God is. It is a response to God, fueled by delight and awe. Furthermore, it is the Spirit of God working in believers that enables us to truly worship and not simply perform outward actions. Jesus also emphasized the importance of worshiping in truth. True worship is a response to who God is, not what we want Him to be. Our worship must be grounded in the truth of who God says He is as revealed in the Bible. Worship involves our heads and our hearts.

Worship is not confined to particular times of the day or week. Believers are called to glorify God in all things, whether it be eating and drinking, working, or enjoying a day at the beach. We are not merely called to insert moments of worship into our lives but to live a life of worship in response to who God is. All people are made in God's image and are called to be His representatives on earth, but sin has marred the image of God in us so that we fall short of His glory. As we grow in godliness and more closely reflect His character, we glorify Him. In Paul's letter to the Romans, he told them that their spiritual act of worship is to offer their bodies as living sacrifices as they become conformed to the image of God. This is a picture of a life lived in service to God and ever-increasing in sanctification. A life of worship is a life of service, obedience, and spiritual growth.

God has graciously revealed Himself to us, and the proper response to His character is worship. God's self-revelation can be broadly categorized as general revelation and special revelation. General revelation is God's revealing of Himself through what He has made. As we see and experience God's creation, we can learn something about the Creator. We can experience His goodness while eating an eclair, feeling the plush grass under our feet, or hearing the sound of ocean waves. We can marvel at His glorious design when we watch a bird build a nest or when we breathe in the smell of lavender or freshly baked chocolate chip cookies. When we enjoy these things with the perspective that every good and perfect gift is from above, looking beyond them to the surpassing beauty of the Creator and His infinite brilliance and artistry, we can worship and adore Him for who He is. God has also revealed Himself through His written Word, the Bible, and through His incarnate Word, Jesus Christ. This kind of revelation is called special revelation, and it is the primary way that God makes Himself known. When we fix our eyes on Christ through the Bible that points to Him, our response should be to worship as we behold His glory.

Worship both proceeds from and accompanies the other spiritual disciplines. We are called to worship in truth, and so God's Word of Truth must be the foundation of our worship. Bible intake, then, is central to a life of worship to God. We are also called to worship in Spirit and move beyond merely intellectual knowledge, and Bible meditation is one means through which the Spirit works to produce that kind of worship. All the spiritual disciplines, from prayer to fasting to fellowship, can all be means of worship and can all lead to deeper worship. We must know God in order to worship Him, and the spiritual disciplines are a means of knowing Him more fully.

All of life should be worship, but it is also important to regularly have intentional times of focused, disciplined worship. We should worship privately through other spiritual disciplines, learning more about who God is and praising Him for His character. It is also important to worship publicly as a part of a local church. The author of Hebrews urges us not to neglect meeting together with other believers for corporate worship. When we gather as a local body of believers, our worship is not confined to the music we sing together, but every element is part of the worship service. We can worship as we sing, hear the reading and preaching of the Word, confess our sins, give, welcome one another, and participate in the Lord's Supper. Each element should facilitate genuine worship as we know and experience Him together. For this reason, the Word of God should be central to the worship service. Private worship and public worship enhance one another, and neither one should be neglected. We grow and mature together in ways that we could not do on our own and vice versa.

Authentic worship takes place in our thoughts, attitudes, and actions. It proceeds from a deep affection for God. Oftentimes, we worship imperfectly. We may find ourselves going through the motions without a sense of joy, delight, or reverence for God. In those times, we must press on. As we continue the disciplines, we must turn to the Lord in prayer and ask Him to soften our hearts to Him. We must continue to gather with fellow believers who will spur us on. The Lord can turn our duty to delight.

To worship God is to glorify Him.

HOW DOES WORSHIP RELATE TO THE OTHER SPIRITUAL DISCIPLINES?

DO YOU TEND TO FOCUS MORE ON PUBLIC WORSHIP OR PRIVATE WORSHIP? HOW CAN YOU BE INTENTIONAL ABOUT INCORPORATING BOTH?

WOULD YOU CHARACTERIZE YOUR CURRENT WORSHIP AS MORE FOCUSED ON SPIRIT OR ON TRUTH?

WEEK 2 MEMORY VERSE

How sweet your word is to my taste—sweeter than honey in my mouth.

—

PSALM 119:103

Week Two Reflection
REVIEW ALL PASSAGES FROM THE WEEK

SUMMARIZE THE MAIN PRINCIPLES YOU LEARNED.

WHAT DID YOU OBSERVE ABOUT GOD'S CHARACTER?

WHAT DID YOU LEARN ABOUT THE CONDITION OF MANKIND AND ABOUT YOURSELF?

HOW WERE YOU POINTED TO THE GOSPEL?

HOW DOES THE GOSPEL ENCOURAGE AND EMPOWER YOU TO PURSUE GODLINESS, AND WHAT SPECIFIC ACTION STEPS CAN YOU TAKE TO IMPLEMENT THE SPIRITUAL DISCIPLINES COVERED THIS WEEK?

WRITE A PRAYER RESPONDING TO WHAT YOU HAVE STUDIED THIS WEEK. ADORE GOD FOR HIS CHARACTER. CONFESS THE SIN THAT HE HAS REVEALED IN YOUR OWN LIFE THIS WEEK. PRAY FOR THOSE WHO THE LORD BROUGHT TO MIND AS YOU STUDIED THIS WEEK.

Week 3 Day 1

"THE SPIRITUAL DISCIPLINE OF PRAYER IS AN OUTWORKING OF KNOWING WHO GOD IS."

PERSONAL PRAYER

Read Matthew 6:5-14, Luke 11:1-13, James 5:13-16

Prayer is a gift. It is an invitation for God's people to commune with Him. As He speaks to His people through His Word, His people are invited to respond back to Him through prayer. The spiritual discipline of prayer is an outworking of knowing who God is. In John 4:10, Jesus tells the Samaritan woman, "If you knew the gift of God, and who is saying to you, 'Give me a drink,' you would ask Him, and He would give you living water." The practice of prayer is fueled by knowing who God is as revealed in His Word. It is in response to knowing Him as the only one who can truly meet all needs. It is in response to knowing Him as a kind and generous giver. It is in response to relating to Him as a child relates to his or her father, in need of His care, provision, and work on his or her behalf.

There are many passages in Scripture that denote the expectation for believers to pray. There are commands to "pray constantly" (1 Thessalonians 5:17) and "devote yourselves to prayer" (Colossians 4:2). There is an implication of prayer being an assumed life posture for the believer. In fact, when believers pray, they are acknowledging their utter dependence on God, which in turn, puts God in His rightful place. And the beautiful thing is, when we behold God as God, we are then further compelled to pray!

Prayer is not a mindless task that must be completed to appease God. While it is something we do, praying is actually participating in sacred communion with God. For believers, prayer should be as natural as breathing. Prayer is a compulsory response to the amazing grace and presence of God in our lives! Yet, many of us reduce prayer to quick sayings before meals or random reflections before drifting off to sleep. Some of us only see the need for deep prayer when we or those we know experience grievous trials. While these elements of expressing thanks, freely conversing, and seeking provision and comfort are valid aspects of prayer, Scripture gives a vision of prayer as a deep devotion of people longing to grow in Christlikeness and as a sacred expression of their union with Him. In prayer, we are actively adoring God for who He is, confessing our sins to Him as we are grieved by the offenses, giving thanks to the giver, expressing deep cries of lament and grief, and seeking comfort from the Comforter, along with wisdom, strength, grace, and more. In prayer, we acknowledge that we need God to do any good thing.

There are many models that offer a systematic framework for prayer, and most of them stem from Jesus' teaching on prayer (Matthew 6, Luke 11). In the Lord's prayer, Jesus offers His disciples a structure to guide their prayers. Because the two accounts in Scripture of the Lord's prayer are not identical, we can deduce that Jesus was setting forth a principle for prayer rather than expecting a rote recitation of the prayer. Jesus offers the Lord's prayer in response to the disciples' request to be taught how to pray. It is clear that prayer is something that is learned. So while prayer is akin to the natural act of breathing for believers, it is a discipline that we must grow in through intentional practice, much like a baby progresses in communicating his or her needs from crying to talking.

The framework in the Lord's prayer is simple: there are God-centered petitions followed by need-centered petitions. The God-centered petitions involve acknowledging God for who He is. He is a relational God, and He is, above all things, worthy of worship. We benefit from beginning our prayers by acknowledging His holiness and adoring Him, because that places us in a posture of humble reverence which then appropriately shapes the rest of our prayers. We want to express our desire for the glory of God to be made known, which is the central goal of the Christian life, before bringing forth our personal requests. We set our eyes on eternity first, knowing that everything else will then fall into proper perspective. This does not mean we shy away from bringing our very real, personal needs before the Lord. Jesus teaches His disciples to bring their physical, emotional, relational, and spiritual needs to the Father. It is right for us to acknowledge that we are needy creatures by God's design. It glorifies God when we look to Him to meet all of our needs.

However, Jesus explicitly teaches how the prayers of His people should not be doused in many words with little meaning. Prayers were not to be reduced to tradition and repetition. Instead, these petitions can be uniquely expounded upon by each believer. Our prayers are deeply personal. We can use our own words, but the beauty is, we are not confined to our own words. We are invited to pray Scripture. We can learn how to pray by reading the prayers of the Puritans. We can journal our prayers. There are many ways to utter our adoration, confession, thanksgiving, and supplication to God. But like Jesus, we consistently seek our secret places to pray alone (Matthew 6:6). No matter our life season, we strive in prayer and endeavor to make communing with the Lord through prayer a daily reality. We make a plan, use the Word of God to guide us, and believe that our prayers are the means that God uses to spiritually prepare us to receive the things He has for us. We trust in His sovereignty but act on the belief that our prayers matter and move the heart of God.

Prayer is a gift.

DESCRIBE YOUR PRAYER LIFE RIGHT NOW. HOW WOULD YOU LIKE YOUR PRAYER LIFE TO MATURE?

WHAT FRAMEWORK FOR PRAYER DOES THE LORD'S PRAYER OFFER US?

IF GOD IS SOVEREIGN, WHY ARE BELIEVERS COMMANDED TO PRAY?

Practical Tips to Help You Pray

There are times when our prayer lives can feel dry, repetitive, or ineffective. We can reduce prayer to be a Christian duty rather than seeing it as an invitation to commune with God. A few things may be helpful. Remember, just because our prayers are personal does not mean we must always use our own words. We are invited to pray God's Words back to Him. It is always helpful to couple our Bible reading and studying time with our prayer time. Simply having a passage of Scripture can guide our prayers and keep our minds on track.

When life is busy, we often do not take the time to think deeply about the condition of our hearts and its implications on our lives. A few prompts are provided in this section. Take time to work through the questions to examine yourself and, if needed, go to the Lord in confession.

PASSAGE: JOHN 15:1-4

I am the true vine, and my Father is the gardener. Every branch in me that does not produce fruit he removes, and he prunes every branch that produces fruit so that it will produce more fruit. You are already clean because of the word I have spoken to you. Remain in me, and I in you. Just as a branch is unable to produce fruit by itself unless it remains on the vine, neither can you unless you remain in me.

PRAYER:

Jesus, You are the true Vine, and by Your grace, I am connected to you, as a branch is connected to a tree. Because I am connected to You, Your Word says that I will bear fruit. And in order to bear much fruit, you will prune away the things in my life that are impediments to this purpose. Even though this process of pruning and growing may be painful, may I rejoice because I am united to You and because the bearing of fruit is Your work in my life. May I abide in you, trusting in Your goodness in my life. May I remain in You, being nurtured and strengthened by Your Word.

QUESTIONS TO PROMPT SELF-EXAMINATION AND ENGAGE IN CONFESSION:

- *What brings me the most joy?*
- *What makes me feel secure or at peace?*
- *What (or to whom) do I turn to when I feel stressed?*
- *What sins am I feeling convicted of right now? Am I justifying any sins?*
- *How do I treat those around me (loved ones, neighbors, and strangers)?*
- *How am I using my gifts and resources? Am I building my own kingdom or His?*
- *How am I using my time and money? What does that say about my beliefs?*
- *How would the world change if all of my current prayers were answered?*
- *What lies have I bought into that are shaping my mind and heart?*
- *What is distracting me from the truth of the gospel and God's mission?*
- *How am I adorning the gospel in my life?*
- *How am I loving those who are marginalized in my local context?*

OTHER HELPFUL RESOURCES:

- Prayer Cards from The Daily Grace Co. (various topics)
- *Thirty-One Days of Prayer Journal* from The Daily Grace Co.
- *All Things New Praying Scripture Journal* from The Daily Grace Co.
- *Scripture for Anxiety Journal* from The Daily Grace Co.
- *The Lord's Prayer* Bible study from The Daily Grace Co.
- *Praying the Bible* by Donald Whitney
- *Praying through the Bible for Your Kids* by Nancy Guthrie
- *Valley of Vision: A Collection of Puritan Prayers and Devotions*

Week 3 Day 2

"AS WE PRAY TOGETHER,
OUR HEARTS ARE KNIT TOGETHER
AS WE SEEK GOD."

CORPORATE PRAYER
Read James 5:16

An important element of a healthy prayer life is corporate prayer. Not only are we called to pray on our own, but we are also commanded to pray with and for others. Scripture is full of examples of the people of God gathering together to pray as one body. When the New Testament church was inaugurated in Acts 2, the Bible says the newly Spirit-filled Christians "devoted themselves to the apostles' teaching, to the fellowship, to the breaking of bread, and to prayer" (Acts 2:42). The apostles prayed over people who were assigned to serve in specific capacities in Acts 6. Paul frequently called upon his readers to pray for him and for other believers. Praying with and for one another is a given for the New Testament church. This spiritual discipline is important to the spiritual health of believers individually and collectively, but it does not happen without intentionality. In order to practice the discipline of praying together, we must first cultivate the discipline of gathering together. Corporate prayer occurs best in the context of relationships formed in a local body of believers.

The best way to establish a discipline of corporate prayer is to consistently attend a church with a regular rhythm of prayer during a weekly worship service. For some churches, corporate prayer looks like a prayer spoken aloud by a pastor or other leader while the congregation prays along silently. In other churches, attenders join together in praying aloud during liturgical movements. Through prayer liturgy, the local body of believers joins together in one voice to proclaim adoration for the Lord, confess sins, and call upon God for help. While there are often gaps in our personal prayer lives, praying structured prayers in a worship gathering causes us to focus our prayers on areas we might otherwise overlook or avoid. As we pray together, our hearts are knit together as we seek God with common praise, common requests, and common confessions. Corporate prayer helps the body of Christ to grow together in love and unity in Him.

In addition to the weekly worship service, praying with others can be especially fruitful in the context of a smaller group. Gatherings of believers like Bible studies and community groups provide space for people to pray together and for one another in a more intimate setting. When we press into a community with the willingness to be vulnerable about our own sins and struggles, we open ourselves up to the opportunity to receive prayer from others, and in turn, to receive healing from our sin and brokenness. The prayers of God's people are powerful, not because of any power they have in themselves but because of the God who answers prayer. The act of praying together, in turn, deepens and strengthens relationships. When we pray for one another, we are committing to the sanctification of our brothers and sisters in Christ, and that commitment carries over into the way that we sacrificially love and serve them. When we are together and when we are apart, believers are called to believe in the power of prayer and out of love to pray on behalf of others.

Like with the other spiritual disciplines, the practice of corporate prayer enriches other areas of our spiritual lives. When we hear others pray, we can often learn a great deal about how to approach God in our own personal prayer. Our hearts are stirred by the outpouring of praise and adoration from a brother or sister to the Lord. The humble confession of a fellow believer can embolden us to be honest about our own sin and pursue holiness. The intercession of another member of the body of Christ can encourage and exhort us to love and care for our neighbors. Like a child develops language from hearing those around him speak, we learn how to converse with God when we witness the conversations of those who have walked with Him as a faithful friend.

We are called to live as the body of Christ, unified in our mission to glorify God as we love Him and love our neighbors, and we cannot walk according to that call without prayer. Living life with fellow sinners in a fallen world brings with it a host of challenges. We need the Holy Spirit to bind us together where sin tears us apart. We must come together in prayer before the Lord who is over all things.

We must come together in prayer before the Lord who is over all things.

IS PRAYING WITH OTHERS COMFORTABLE OR UNCOMFORTABLE FOR YOU?

TAKE A MOMENT TO WRITE A PRAYER BELOW FOR SOMEONE THAT YOU HAVE COMMITTED TO PRAY FOR OR WHO IS ON YOUR MIND. AFTER YOU WRITE THE PRAYER, SEND THEM A MESSAGE LETTING THEM KNOW YOU PRAYED FOR THEM.

HOW CAN YOU INTENTIONALLY PURSUE COMMUNITY WHERE REGULAR PRAYER TAKES PLACE?

Week 3 Day 3

"THE REGULAR FELLOWSHIP
WITH OTHER BELIEVERS IS A MEANS
OF GOD'S GRACE IN OUR LIVES."

FELLOWSHIP OF BELIEVERS

Read Romans 6:1-11, Matthew 26:26-28, 1 Peter 1:14-22

A survey of the overall story of Scripture shows God always in pursuit of His people. This is because God covenanted to save a people for Himself before sin even entered the world. God created His image-bearers out of an overflow of perfect love and fellowship experienced within the Godhead (the Father, the Son, and Holy Spirit), and this will be fully realized at the consummation when His people will be gathered together and live in His presence in the new heaven and new earth (Revelation 21). Believers, while invited to a personal relationship with God through Christ, experience God more fully when they are part of a church. In His infinite wisdom, He created us to live out our faith in a communal way, collectively as His people. Until Jesus returns, we have the gift of fellowship of Christian believers! David declared in Psalm 133:1, "How delightfully good when brothers live together in harmony!" Like the other spiritual disciplines, living together in harmony with fellow believers is something we do, and the regular fellowship with other believers is a means of God's grace in our lives.

We can see that the early church devoted themselves to daily fellowship (Acts 2:42). Meeting together as a church is important. But we may wonder what Christian fellowship should look like today. There are a few defining activities that believers do within the context of the local church that are uniquely important, and they are called ordinances. These ordinances—baptism and the Lord's Supper—visibly distinguish the community of believers that make up the church. These ordinances are explicitly found in Scripture, and they are far richer than mere Christian tradition or religious ritual. These ordinances are outward expressions of the inward disposition of our union with Christ.

Baptism and partaking of the Lord's Supper were both ordained by Jesus for the edification of His body. In Matthew 28:19-20, Jesus commanded His disciples, "Go, therefore, and make disciples of all nations, baptizing them in the name of the Father and of the Son and of the Holy Spirit, teaching them to observe everything I have commanded you." Baptism is a command for every believer. The Holy Spirit affirms this through the Apostle Peter in Acts 2:38 when Peter says, "Repent and be baptized, each of you, in the name of Jesus Christ for the forgiveness of your sins, and you will receive the gift of the Holy Spirit." Thus, when a believer is baptized, he or she is acting in obedience to God. Furthermore, the physical act of baptism is symbolic of one's spiritual reality; it is a visible symbol of repentance in the believer's heart. In baptism, we are outwardly displaying the inward transformation of dying to sin and being raised to a new life in Christ. The water also represents this cleansing from sin that comes through the life, death, and resurrection of Christ. This particular way of publicly confessing our union with Christ is typically only done once, but it is affirmed regularly through the partaking of the Lord's Supper (also known as communion).

Jesus is also the one who instituted the Lord's Supper. In 1 Corinthians 11:24-25, He offers the bread and wine to His disciples as symbols of His body and "the new covenant in [His] blood." Today, believers regularly partake in the Lord's Supper in remembrance of Christ and His death, burial, and resurrection. While the Bible does not specify the frequency of the Lord's Supper (hence, some churches offer communion weekly while others do so monthly), it is a regular practice seen within the fellowship of the early church. Partaking in the Lord's Supper is an essential component of Christian fellowship.

Together, these ordinances are expressions of the new birth that believers have in Christ. In Christ, we are children of God. This is now our identity, and this new birth leads to new life. We see that 1 Peter 1:14-22 expounds on this when it says we are called to holiness because we are "redeemed from your empty way of life." And as obedient children, we are to love one another constantly with a pure heart (1 Peter 1:22). Christian fellowship is an overflow of being children of God. It is the outward sign of a shared, inward reality. We, as Christians, ought to live differently because we are different. Our fellowship is not like the world's—it goes beyond shared interests, causes, and passions. Christian fellowship is an expression of hearts and minds united by the gospel of Jesus. Our union with Christ also unites us to one another. This is why Christian fellowship enjoys true unity within diversity. It is not about our ethnicities, financial situations, political views, family make-ups, social convictions, etc. It is about Jesus and together, being His people. This fellowship involves sharing in each other's sufferings and carrying one another's burdens. It involves confessing our sins to one another, extending the grace of Jesus to one another, and reminding each other of the gospel. It involves opening our hearts and our homes to those around us, adorning the unifying power of the gospel.

Christian fellowship requires intentionality. It requires a commitment to be an active member of the body of Christ. Perhaps this deep fellowship develops within the context of a small group in the local church where a number of believers regularly meet to study Scripture, pray, and share their lives together. Maybe it happens in the context of a Sunday school class. Regardless, Christian fellowship requires effort, vulnerability, and authenticity rooted in the truth of the gospel. As believers, we live as exiles in this world together, and we live in such a way that testifies to the truth that we are anticipating the return of Christ.

He created us to live out our faith in a communal way.

IF OUR FAITH IS A PERSONAL RELATIONSHIP WITH GOD THROUGH CHRIST, WHAT IS THE BENEFIT OF ENGAGING IN FELLOWSHIP WITH OTHER BELIEVERS?

WHAT DO BAPTISM AND THE LORD'S SUPPER SIGNIFY?

HOW IS CHRISTIAN FELLOWSHIP DIFFERENT FROM THE WORLD'S IDEA OF FELLOWSHIP BETWEEN DIFFERENT GROUPS OF PEOPLE?

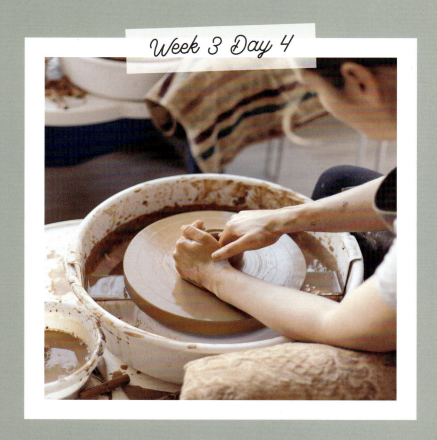

Week 3 Day 4

"ALL BELIEVERS ARE CALLED TO SERVE IN A WAY THAT IS SACRIFICIAL."

SERVING

Read Matthew 25:35-40, John 13:12-16, 1 Corinthians 12:4-27, Ephesians 4:15-16

The Christian life is a life of costly service. All believers are called to serve in a way that is sacrificial. In the busyness of life, service can easily be pushed aside, and just like we must intentionally make time to exercise or read our Bibles, we must discipline ourselves to serve. As believers, we serve God, not to earn salvation but because we have been lavished with grace. Service to God is the joyous and grateful response of believers who have understood how Christ has so sacrificially served them. The Son of God became a man in order to save sinners from death, serving all the way to the point of an excruciating and shameful death. We are called to imitate His example and are compelled by His love to give of ourselves. When we serve from a place of forgiveness instead of an attempt to earn forgiveness, our service will no longer be characterized by guilt or drudgery but by gratitude and gladness.

Jesus said in Matthew 22 that the greatest commandment is to love God, and the second greatest is to love our neighbors. Our willingness to serve is empowered by our love for God, and love for God is accompanied by love for our neighbor. When we love God, we love like God. The other spiritual disciplines are vitally important for sustaining a life of service because it is through them that our affection for God grows. If we separate service from a deepening love for God cultivated through Bible intake, prayer, and other disciplines, our service will be motivated by guilt or by a desire to gain praise, recognition, or influence. If we ever find these kinds of motivations on our hearts, we must turn to God in repentance and preach the gospel to our own hearts, remembering the length that Christ went to serve us.

We were never meant to live this life alone. God created us to live in community, serving one another as we serve God. Scripture describes the people of God using metaphors such as parts of a body or stones in a building. The individual parts make up the whole and cannot function properly without one another. Every member of the body of Christ has been given at least one spiritual gift—a gift empowered by the Holy Spirit—for the good of the body. One person may have the gift of teaching while another has the gift of leadership. Whatever the gifts, they are given, not for the sake of the person who has the gift but for the sake of others. Every believer should find a way to serve in the local church as a means to build up the body of Christ using his or her own gift. It is also important to realize that not all types of serving require a specific spiritual gift, and whether or not we particularly enjoy a certain type of service should not necessarily be the determining factor in whether or not we serve in that capacity. While someone with a gift of teaching would be best suited to teach a Sunday school class, a specific spiritual gift is not required to wash dishes after a church event.

In addition to serving in the context of the local church, we should serve those in our home as well as our neighbors. Serving in the home could look like teaching and discipling children, creating a clean and welcoming environment, preparing meals, or working to bring income into the home. Service to those in our home should not be purely out of duty but out of love and a desire to care for those around us. Serving also extends to our neighbors in countless ways. This kind of service could mean welcoming others into our homes and sharing the love of Christ with them through hospitality. It could look like making a meal for someone who is struggling or volunteering to tutor students at a local school. As we serve others with a happy heart, we put on display the love that Christ freely offers.

Service benefits others, but it also causes us to grow in spiritual maturity and Christlikeness. As we serve, we can constantly call to mind the way Christ served us, growing in our love and affection for Him, which in turn leads to a desire to serve. We become increasingly like Jesus as we serve sacrificially, empowered by the Spirit within us.

The Christian life is a life of costly service.

WHAT DOES JOHN 13:12-26 REVEAL ABOUT WHAT SHOULD MOTIVATE OUR SERVICE?

READ MARK 10:45. WHERE DO YOU SEE A DESIRE TO BE SERVED IN YOUR LIFE INSTEAD OF TO SERVE, WHETHER IN THE CONTEXT OF THE HOME, THE LOCAL CHURCH, OR SOMEWHERE ELSE?

WHAT SPECIFIC NEEDS CAN YOU MEET IN YOUR CHURCH, HOME, AND COMMUNITY?

Week 3 Day 5

"EVANGELISM, SIMPLY PUT, IS PRESENTING THE GOSPEL TO UNBELIEVERS IN HOPES THAT THEY MIGHT BELIEVE AND BE SAVED."

EVANGELISM

Read Matthew 28:18-20, 1 Peter 2:9-10

Practicing spiritual disciplines helps us to mature as believers of Christ and grow in godliness, but they are also for the benefit of others. Evangelism and discipleship are spiritual disciplines focusing on the salvation and maturity of others, while also helping us to grow in godliness. Evangelism, simply put, is presenting the gospel to unbelievers in hopes that they might believe and be saved. Evangelism can take many forms, from a conversation with a neighbor to a sermon delivered before thousands of people. Discipleship is an ongoing relationship in which a believer walks alongside a newer believer or even an unbeliever. Discipleship, then, can be a means of evangelism, but it goes beyond gospel presentation to seek spiritual maturity.

All believers are commanded to share the gospel. In Matthew 28, Jesus commanded His disciples to take the message of the gospel to all nations. This command is continued for all believers, and even now there are parts of the world that are still unreached by the gospel. All who believe in Christ are part of a royal priesthood called to be mediators of the message of salvation to an unbelieving world, always proclaiming the praises of the One who saved us (1 Peter 2:9-10). While opportunities for evangelism can sometimes arise spontaneously, if we are to practice evangelism regularly, we must discipline ourselves to do so.

Evangelism can take place in a variety of contexts and through a variety of methods. We may evangelize over coffee with an unbelieving friend, by sharing our testimony at a church event, or even in writing. Regardless of the method of delivery, evangelism must include the truth of the gospel being clearly stated. The way we live our lives is an important element of our evangelism, as Jesus commanded His disciples to live in such a way that those around them would see their good deeds and in turn glorify God (Matthew 5:16). Our actions matter, but living out the gospel is not enough. Evangelism requires that the essential elements of the gospel message be proclaimed, and the transforming power of that gospel is evidenced by our conduct.

Evangelism may seem daunting, but understanding our role in evangelism can help to relieve some pressure. When it comes to evangelism, our responsibility is to accurately present the truth of the gospel, and God is the one who brings about transformation. We have no power to change hearts or produce faith, and so the success of our evangelism is not contingent upon conversion but upon whether or not the good news of Jesus Christ was proclaimed. Every believer has the tools necessary to evangelize: a basic understanding of the gospel message and the indwelling Holy Spirit who empowers us to speak. Evangelism does not require a seminary degree, giftedness in speaking and teaching, or an outgoing personality. Every person who has been transformed by the gospel is equipped to proclaim the excellencies of Christ. Part of the discipline of evangelism is seeking out times and ways to do it. We must be intentional about spending time with unbelievers, caring for them through service, praying for them, and asking questions that can lead to gospel conversations.

Discipleship goes beyond proclaiming the hope of the gospel to unbelievers and seeks to walk alongside someone on their journey of sanctification. The word "disciple" means follower. In a discipleship relationship, one person leads another through a book of the Bible or elements of Christian faith and living. These relationships are incredibly important because the disciple learns not only from the words of the one who disciples but from his or her witness of conduct. It is a type of spiritual mentorship with the goal of sanctification. The less experienced person in the relationship is not the only one who grows from this experience, but the more seasoned believer will also be formed into Christlikeness. This kind of relationship involves learning together, praying for one another, encouraging each other, and holding one another accountable.

The other spiritual disciplines play an important role in discipleship and evangelism. Through them we gain a greater knowledge of God and His Word, giving us confidence and fluency to present the gospel effectively. Through the disciplines, we grow in our love for God, making us more eager to proclaim His goodness. Because of the disciplines, we grow in love for the body of Christ and our neighbors so that our desire to share the gospel with them will be genuine. The goal of spiritual disciplines is godliness, and a life that reflects the hope we are proclaiming through discipleship and evangelism is a powerful witness to those who hear.

The goal of spiritual disciplines is godliness.

READ ACTS 1:8. WHAT EMPOWERS EVANGELISM AND MAKES IT EFFECTIVE? HOW DOES THIS IMPACT THE WAY YOU VIEW EVANGELISM?

RECALL A TIME WHEN YOU HAVE BEEN DISCIPLED BY SOMEONE, WHETHER FORMALLY OR INFORMALLY. WHAT IMPACT DID THAT RELATIONSHIP HAVE ON YOUR LIFE?

1 PETER 3:15 ENCOURAGES US TO BE READY TO GIVE A REASON FOR THE HOPE THAT IS IN US. IF THE OPPORTUNITY AROSE FOR YOU TO SHARE THE GOSPEL, WHAT WOULD YOU SAY? WRITE OUT A SHORT PRESENTATION OF THE GOSPEL THAT YOU COULD PRACTICE FOR SUCH TIMES.

WEEK 3 MEMORY VERSE

But speaking the truth in love, let us grow in every way into him who is the head—Christ. From him the whole body, fitted and knit together by every supporting ligament, promotes the growth of the body for building itself up in love by the proper working of each individual part.

—

EPHESIANS 4:15-16

Week Three Reflection

REVIEW ALL PASSAGES FROM THE WEEK

SUMMARIZE THE MAIN PRINCIPLES YOU LEARNED.

WHAT DID YOU OBSERVE ABOUT GOD'S CHARACTER?

WHAT DID YOU LEARN ABOUT THE CONDITION OF MANKIND AND ABOUT YOURSELF?

HOW WERE YOU POINTED TO THE GOSPEL?

HOW DOES THE GOSPEL ENCOURAGE AND EMPOWER YOU TO PURSUE GODLINESS, AND WHAT SPECIFIC ACTION STEPS CAN YOU TAKE TO IMPLEMENT THE SPIRITUAL DISCIPLINES COVERED THIS WEEK?

WRITE A PRAYER RESPONDING TO WHAT YOU HAVE STUDIED THIS WEEK. ADORE GOD FOR HIS CHARACTER. CONFESS THE SIN THAT HE HAS REVEALED IN YOUR OWN LIFE THIS WEEK. PRAY FOR THOSE WHO THE LORD BROUGHT TO MIND AS YOU STUDIED THIS WEEK.

Week 4 Day 1

"WHEN A BELIEVER FASTS, HE OR SHE IS SAYING 'NO' TO GOOD GIFTS GIVEN FROM GOD IN ORDER TO SAY 'YES' TO GOD HIMSELF."

FASTING

Read Matthew 6:16-18, Matthew 9:14-17

Fasting is not unique to Christianity. The practice of abstaining from food transcends world religions and cultures. There are people who use it as a means to lose weight or make a social or political point. However, Christian fasting has spiritual purposes that are rooted in the Word of God. While not explicitly commanded in Scripture, there are many passages that reveal an expectation that God's people would fast. In the Sermon on the Mount in Matthew 6, Jesus taught on various topics like giving, praying, and fasting. In each of these instances, He used the phrase, "when you" (Matthew 6:3, 6-7, 17). Jesus assumed His disciples would do these things. Yet, Christian fasting in particular is a spiritual discipline that is widely misunderstood and neglected amongst believers.

In the Bible, a normal fast is depicted as abstaining from food but not water. However, there are various forms of fasting seen throughout Scripture. Jesus never set forth rigid parameters for a fast like how long, how often, and from what. Thus, it is more beneficial to consider the spiritual purposes behind fasting. What gain comes from abstaining from things for a period of time—things, for the most part, which are not inherently bad in and of themselves? How does fasting deepen one's communion with God?

The discipline of fasting does many things in and for the believer. In a broad sense, when a believer fasts, he or she is saying "no" to good gifts given from God in order to say "yes" to God Himself. This can be difficult. When food is foregone, hunger pangs come. When social media is surrendered, the temptation to scroll is heightened. Feelings of anger, anxiety, fear, impatience or boredom may arise. Suddenly, we are made aware of the places we have found satisfaction, validation, and purpose. The preferences and affections of our hearts are brought to the surface.

This is why fasting is a way for believers to echo Paul's words from 1 Corinthians 6:12. In purposefully foregoing certain things for a period of time, we are declaring, "'Everything is permissible for me,' but not everything is beneficial. 'Everything is permissible for me,' but I will not be mastered by anything." It is a means of grace for believers because it invites us to see the things we have been mastered by, and in turn, run to the Lord in repentance. While we fast, we simultaneously pray that our affection for Christ would grow to be far superior to anything else. We intentionally withhold good things from ourselves in order to take hold of the better portion. Instead of feasting on the pleasures of this world, we allow our hearts to hunger for God more intensely, reminding ourselves that He alone can truly satisfy us. In this way, fasting is a means to help us lean into our anticipation for the return of Christ.

Ultimately, we fast because we are awaiting the return of Jesus. When Jesus came, He inaugurated His kingdom. However, we are still waiting on its consummation which will happen when He returns. In this time of waiting, it is appropriate for believers to fast. Jesus eluded to this in Matthew 9:15. Jesus was responding to the Pharisees when they asked why His disciples were not following the Jewish tradition of participating in weekly fasts. Jesus said, "Can the wedding guests be sad while the groom is with them? The time will come when the groom will be taken away from them, and then they will fast." That time has come. We, the bridegroom of Christ, are in a season of waiting for the return of our groom.

Fasting reminds us that this is not our home. The emptiness in our stomachs is a tangible way to feel the emptiness of this world. Christians are not called to ignore the emptiness of this world. The goal is not to fill the emptiness by our own means. The aim is to remind ourselves and remind others that Jesus is the only one who can fill our emptiness. This emptiness can look like many different things including infertility, broken marriages, loneliness, anxiety, depression, addictions, or the death of loved ones, and more. Whatever it may be, Jesus is the answer, and fasting is a time to lean into that truth. It is a means to deepen our hunger for God and stifle our appetites for the lesser things this world has to offer.

Fasting can be done regularly or in times of crisis. It can be done corporately or privately. However, in our times of fasting, may we do it in such a way to glorify God. May we not engage in this spiritual discipline to make ourselves look or feel more spiritual, but may it be a means of grace to cultivate a greater affection for God.

Ultimately, we fast because we are awaiting the return of Jesus.

WHAT ARE THE SPIRITUAL BENEFITS OF CHRISTIAN FASTING?

WHEN WE ENGAGE IN FASTING, WHAT ARE WE COMMUNICATING TO GOD?

IS THERE SOMETHING YOU CAN ABSTAIN FROM FOR A PERIOD OF TIME THAT WOULD INCREASE YOUR HUNGER FOR GOD AND DEEPEN YOUR COMMUNION WITH HIM? WHAT IS IT?

Week 4 Day 2

"A DAILY DISCIPLINE OF SILENCE AND SOLITUDE CAN FACILITATE SIGNIFICANT SPIRITUAL GROWTH."

SILENCE AND SOLITUDE

Read Psalm 62, Mark 1:35

Contemporary life is characterized by busyness and noise. For some, a moment alone is hard to come by, and there is no bit of silence to be found. When we do have a quiet moment alone, we are often quick to fill it by habitually reaching for a phone, busying ourselves with some task, or turning on music or the television as background noise. To practice silence and solitude is to intentionally withdraw for a time, uninterrupted by people, noise, or social media. The spiritual disciplines of silence and solitude are largely countercultural, but they can provide fruitful benefits for the believer.

Jesus was a man who gave fully of Himself. He served sacrificially, teaching, healing, and even dying for the sake of others. Even so, Jesus habitually withdrew to a quiet place alone. Scripture says that He prayed in desolate places, rising early in the morning or departing from crowds in order to experience solitude. If we desire to grow in Christlikeness, we must follow His example.

Practicing silence and solitude may sound appealing to some and dreadful to others. Either way, spending time alone in silence is more challenging than we may think. We may find ourselves reaching to check our phones almost involuntarily within just minutes or even seconds of uninterrupted silence. For some, being alone with our thoughts can seem almost unbearable. In the quiet moments alone we are forced to face our fears, our doubt, and our shame. Perhaps we fear that total silence and isolation will confirm our fear that we are actually alone. So we fill the silence with music or podcasts. We seek company in the voices on TV or a social media feed. Anything to avoid silence and make us feel less alone.

Intentionally and regularly practicing silence and solitude provides space for busy minds to be quieted to make room for practices that contribute to spiritual growth. Without people or noise to drown out the pangs of conviction, we are able to see our sin more clearly and confess it to God who promises to "forgive us our sins and to cleanse us from all unrighteousness" (1 John 1:9). Silence and solitude make way for other spiritual disciplines like Bible study, meditation, and prayer to be practiced without distraction so that they cannot merely be outward actions but disciplines done from the heart. All the spiritual disciplines are a means to godliness, and silence and solitude provide a focused place and time to practice them.

1 Chronicles 16:11 calls us to "Seek the Lord and his strength; seek his face always." Without disciplining ourselves to practice silence and solitude, we can find ourselves forgetting to seek the Lord at all. When we cut off the noise and retreat to a quiet place, our tendency to fill the space with distractions can be replaced by reaching out to God. When we see God in lonely places, without noise or distraction, we will find that we are not alone at all. The awareness of His presence as we draw near to Him spills over into the rest of our lives, and we will likely find ourselves calling out to Him in the busy and overwhelming moments when we seek Him in the quiet ones.

In Psalm 62, David seeks the Lord from a place of silence. He waits on the Lord in confidence that He alone is his refuge, his rock, and his salvation. When we come to God in silence, we can press into Him, confident that our hope is in Him alone and not in people, not in our work, and not in entertainment. David invites us to pour out our hearts before God. We often seek to numb our pain through distractions, but God invites us to feel it all and lay it all before Him because He is a safe place. He is a refuge and a strong tower.

A daily discipline of silence and solitude can facilitate significant spiritual growth. Silence and solitude is a way of practicing in quiet and stillness what we should exhibit in busyness and noise. In silence and solitude, we practice being slow to speak and quick to listen (James 1:19). We practice resting in God and not in our work. We practice turning to God and seeking His face instead of looking for comfort elsewhere.

He is a refuge and a strong tower.

WHAT ARE YOUR FEARS SURROUNDING THE PRACTICE OF SILENCE AND SOLITUDE?

WHAT ARE SOME BARRIERS TO THE PRACTICE OF SILENCE AND SOLITUDE IN YOUR LIFE? WHAT PRACTICAL STEPS CAN YOU TAKE TO MAKE SPACE FOR THIS DISCIPLINE?

HOW MIGHT A REGULAR PRACTICE OF SILENCE AND SOLITUDE CHANGE THE WAY YOU GO THROUGHOUT THE REST OF YOUR DAY?

Week 4 Day 3

"BIBLICAL STEWARDSHIP IS USING EVERYTHING WE HAVE FOR THE PURPOSES OF CHRIST."

STEWARDSHIP

Read Matthew 25:14-30

All of the spiritual disciplines are things believers actively do. They are ways in which we pursue holiness and train ourselves up in godliness (1 Timothy 4:7). The more we understand how the gospel changes everything, the more we understand that every aspect of our lives can be devoted to this pursuit of holiness. All of our lives can be training grounds for growing in godliness. This is why the way we spend our time, resources, and talents is important. We believe these things were entrusted to us, and stewarding them well is a spiritual discipline.

Understanding stewardship from a biblical worldview begins with the gospel because the gospel reminds us that everything we have has been given to us by God (1 Corinthians 4:7). The gospel offers us right standing before God, transforming our relationship with Him. Salvation is a gift from God (Ephesians 2:8). The gospel also transforms how we relate to everything else in our lives. This is what happens when people seek first the Kingdom of God—everything else is impacted. Following Jesus has radical implications for our lives.

We know that, in His infinite wisdom, God specifically apportioned gifts to His people. Each of us is given specific gifts and in specific measures. Nothing we have (talents, abilities, resources, etc.) is by accident or even of our own doing. They are varied measures of His grace, and we are meant to be good stewards of what He has given us, using our gifts to serve others (1 Peter 4:10). Our individual gifts are given to us by God for the common good (1 Corinthians 12:7). They are not measures of favor nor the means to bolster personal image or worth. Those of us who are united to Christ are "no longer foreigners and strangers, but fellow citizens with the saints, and members of God's household" (Ephesians 2:19). Through our union with Christ, we are children of God, wholly loved and accepted by the Father. Our identities are in Christ, and it is from this place of security that we live our lives.

Biblical stewardship is using everything we have for the purposes of Christ. This includes using our spiritual gifts in the church for the edification of the body and using our talents and abilities in the home and in the workplace for the glory of God. This also prompts us to ask ourselves, "How can the way we give and spend our money further the purposes of Christ?" There is no universal formula to this. In fact, biblical stewardship goes beyond the abandonment of material goods and worldly comforts. Instead, it is anchored in Jesus' call to count the cost of following Him and upon counting the cost, to understand what He means when He says, "every one of you who does not renounce all his possessions cannot be my disciple" (Luke 14:33). This is a call to total surrender. It is refusing to hold on tightly to any earthly possession, secret indulgence, or personal sins. Instead, it is striving to obey the Lord and His Word, no matter the cost.

A total commitment to Christ beckons us to pay close attention to how we are living. Paul admonishes believers to "pay careful attention" to how we live our lives, "making the most of the time, because the days are evil" (Ephesians 5:15-

16). Time is a priceless commodity that each of us should strive to steward well. Every moment matters for eternity. So we want to discipline ourselves. We can ask these questions: What thoughts are we spending time mulling over? What are we watching and listening to? How much time are we devoting to entertainment? What are we investing ourselves in most? Are laziness and mindless distractions a normal part of our days?

The goal of biblical stewardship is not for believers to look absolutely identical. How we spend our time, money, resources, and talents will look differently. However, the impetus is the same: the gospel. The gospel unites us in our cause — to glorify God — and it does this in the midst of our diverse gifts, financial situations, life circumstances, and more. The discipline of stewardship is exercised knowing that the days are evil. There are so many different things vying for our attention and our hearts' affections. It does not take much effort to waste time. Thus, stewardship of our time and everything else is very much a discipline that we need to intentionally and consistently exercise.

Biblical stewardship is not easy. We need the Spirit's help. The answer is not to flex our own willpower. The answer is Jesus. We need His strength. We need Him to transform our hearts and minds and desires. We need to do the hard work of seeking first His kingdom, and this begins by seeing the supreme value of knowing and being known by Christ. May our affection for God surpass everything else this world has to offer. May we not forget that each of us will have to give an account to God (Romans 14:12, 1 Corinthians 3:13-15, Matthew 12:36, Matthew 25:14-30). So may we handle all of the things entrusted to us in such a way that it is abundantly clear on that day that we were totally committed and surrendered to the person of Christ, His glory, and His purposes.

The gospel unites us in our cause.

READ I CORINTHIANS 12:4-11. OUR SPIRITUAL GIFTS AND VARIOUS TALENTS AND ABILITIES ARE GIFTED TO US BY GOD FOR THE GOOD OF OTHERS. HOW DOES THIS CHANGE THE WAY YOU VIEW YOUR PARTICULAR GIFTS? HOW DOES IT CHANGE THE WAY YOU VIEW OTHER PEOPLE'S GIFTS?

WHAT AREA OF YOUR LIFE DO YOU STRUGGLE WITH THE MOST TO USE FOR THE PURPOSES OF CHRIST? TAKE SOME TIME TO PRAY OVER THOSE AREAS.

WHAT WOULD STEWARDSHIP OF YOUR TIME, TALENTS, AND RESOURCES LOOK LIKE THAT WOULD CLEARLY TELL OTHERS THAT YOU ARE COMMITTED AND SURRENDERED TO JESUS, HIS GLORY, AND HIS PURPOSES?

Week 4 Day 4

"THE GOSPEL IS THE
STARTING POINT FOR CULTIVATING
A HEART OF GRATITUDE."

GIVING THANKS AND REJOICING ALWAYS

Read Psalm 32:1-2, Psalm 118

The gospel is good news. When Jesus was born, the angels declared His arrival as "good news of great joy that will be for all the people" (Luke 2:10). Jesus is precious for countless reasons. He is the Messiah who the Redeemer promised in Genesis 3. He is the Word, full of grace and truth (John 1:1). He is "the way, the truth, and the life" (John 14:6). In His presence is abundant joy, and with Him are eternal pleasures (Psalm 16:11). When the eyes of our hearts are enlightened, we are enabled to see Christ for who He is, and our hearts are filled with wonder.

This wonder for the person of Christ is a gift for believers. It is the motivation behind every single spiritual discipline. As we see the beauty of Christ and enjoy intimacy with Him, we are motivated to feast on His Word, engage with His body, and worship with our lives. He is the reason why the Christian life is a joy-filled life. He is why gratitude and joy are to be our consistent disposition. Scripture actually commands us to give thanks at all times; in fact, gratitude is God's will for His people (1 Thessalonians 5:18). We are also instructed to rejoice at all times (Philippians 4:4). But is this possible? If so, how? On this side of eternity, we must engage in the spiritual disciplines of giving thanks and rejoicing in all circumstances.

In the Old Testament, God's people were instructed to faithfully observe certain feasts every year. These feasts were invitations for His people to remember and rejoice in God's goodness, faithfulness, and provision. They were times to gather with others and celebrate God, His work, and their identity as His people. While these feasts are not required observances for believers today, the principle of gathering together as God's people remains essential in order to remember and rejoice in who God is. In this way, the spiritual disciplines of celebrating and giving thanks are corporate in nature.

These disciplines can and should be practiced in private as well. Often, we will find that a large part of cultivating a grateful heart and joyful spirit is removing hindrances to our joy in the Lord. These hindrances can be anything causing us to forget the gospel. The gospel is the starting point for cultivating a heart of gratitude. It is knowing deep in our souls that we are sinners and justly deserving of death, but God, out of His great love and mercy for us, gave us life. The gospel compels us to be grateful in every season. The gospel is what removes our sense of entitlement. And the gospel is our reason for abundant joy in the Lord. We are now alive together with Christ (Ephesians 2:5).

Not only are we made alive in Christ, but we are now empowered to walk in this newness of life. We have the indwelling Spirit, and it is the Spirit who gives us the ability to see the goodness and love of God, to remember His faithfulness, and to rejoice in His provision. The ability to live "overflowing with gratitude" in every circumstance is to be "rooted and built up in [Christ] and established in the faith" (Colossians 2:7). And being rooted, built up, and established in the faith requires sound doctrine. In this way, the other spiritual disciplines can be fuel for the spiritual disciplines of giving thanks and rejoicing always. And in turn, the spirit of gratitude and celebration encourages us in the continual pursuit of the other disciplines.

Having sound doctrine does not mean we have to be serious all the time. Instead, knowing God and being filled with His Spirit should compel us to shout for joy. When we consider the work of God, we cannot help but rejoice. This is seen all throughout Scripture. God's people are commanded to sing for joy; they are often depicted as singing and dancing in response to who God is and what He is doing. The same should be true of us. How can we not be overflowing with gratitude and joy when we are united to Christ, the victorious one? How can we not be marked by deep gratitude and abounding joy when we are recipients of His redeeming and restoring grace? In response to our union with Christ and His sustaining grace, we joyfully walk in obedience to His Word and experience the multiplication of our joy as a result. We preach the gospel to ourselves, refusing to allow familiarity with its truths to breed indifference.

This does not mean that our lives are easy. This does not mean that we are not allowed to grieve the brokenness of this world or lament. This simply means that our joy is anchored in something—Someone—beyond this world. Our gratitude and our joy are not dependent on our ever-changing circumstances but on the unchanging person of Jesus Christ. In engaging in the spiritual disciplines of giving thanks and rejoicing always, we are rehearsing for the future that is ours with Christ in eternity.

The gospel is good news.

HOW DOES THE GOSPEL COMPEL US TO GIVE THANKS AT ALL TIMES AND TO REJOICE ALWAYS?

WHAT IS ACTING AS A HINDRANCE TO YOUR JOY IN THE LORD TODAY? ARE THERE THINGS IN YOUR LIFE THAT CAUSE YOU TO FORGET THE GOSPEL ON A DAILY BASIS?

BECAUSE OF CHRIST, GRATITUDE AND JOY CAN BE OUR STEADY DISPOSITION, BUT THIS DOES NOT MEAN WE CANNOT GRIEVE OR LAMENT OVER THE BROKENNESS OF THIS WORLD. HOW DO THESE DIFFERENT EMOTIONAL STATES OF BEING CO-EXIST IN THE LIFE OF A BELIEVER? READ I THESSALONIANS 4:13-14 FOR AN EXAMPLE.

Week 4 Day 5

"HE ENABLES US TO REMAIN FAITHFUL. HE PROMISES TO FINISH THE GOOD WORK HE STARTED IN US."

PERSEVERANCE

Read Philippians 2:12-18, 2 Peter 1:3-11, Hebrews 2:1-13

The Christian life is a happy life, but it does not come without work. Growing in godliness does not passively happen in the lives of believers. Though we are given the righteousness of Christ in and through our union with Him, this is only the beginning of our experience of our new birth. Throughout the New Testament, we see this call for believers to live in a way that is consistent with their new identities as children of God. In Ephesians 4:1-3, Paul urges fellow believers "to live worthy of the calling [they] have received, with all humility and gentleness, with patience, bearing with one another in love, making every effort to keep the unity of the Spirit through the bond of peace." Paul gives this exhortation to the church in Colossae as well (Colossians 1:10-12). There, Paul reminds believers that their endurance is a result of God's glorious might which strengthens them with all power. Although engaging in the spiritual disciplines both personally and corporately takes intentional effort and even vigilance, we are not left without God's help. He enables us to remain faithful. He promises to finish the good work He started in us (Philippians 1:6).

But we have work to do, too. While we do not earn our salvation by good works, we are called to "work out [our] own salvation with fear and trembling" (Philippians 2:12). This is the call to be in active pursuit of obedience to God and His Word. This is our part in our sanctification. This is the pursuit of godliness and the why behind the spiritual disciplines. But if we are honest, it is not always easy. There are so many things vying for our attention and energy. And this work is not always glamorous. For the most part, the work is unseen, and the fruit is not always evident right away. But there is value in the ordinary, everyday faithfulness. Persevering to the end is necessary.

Perseverance in the lifelong pursuit of growing in godliness requires daily decisions to discipline ourselves. Growing in holiness does not involve a one-time commitment to follow Christ. It requires a daily commitment to follow Him. This is exactly what Jesus says in Luke 9:23—"If anyone wants to follow after me, let him deny himself, take up his cross daily, and follow me." Our cross to bear is not a life merely of self-denial, completely void of joy. In fact, it is the opposite. Our cross to pick up daily is the willingness to, day in and day out, obey His commands, love and serve others, and do all things for His glory. It is a life of emptying ourselves and being filled with Christ. This kind of life leads to inexpressible joy.

We can hold two truths in tension. Jesus said the narrow way is difficult (Matthew 7:14), but He also said, "For my yoke is easy and my burden is light" (Matthew 11:30). Following Jesus and being faithful every day are not natural inclinations of our sinful hearts. Turning away from our sins in repentance, submitting our lives to the lordship of Christ, and obeying His Word only happens when the gospel transforms our hearts, minds, and wills. We cannot do it apart from Christ. This is why we need to be tethered to Him. We are invited to take His yoke and learn from Him who is gentle and lowly in heart. And as we work, we will find rest for our souls.

The hope in engaging in spiritual disciplines is not to reach a level of mastery that will then allow us to coast. Being tethered to Christ and walking the narrow way is actually a way of life. It is a trajectory on which we remain. As branches attached to the true Vine (John 15), we cannot attach and detach whenever we feel like it. When we are grafted into His family by His grace through faith, we cannot help but be changed. And it is through this steadfast connection that we bear fruit or do anything good. Genuine union with Christ begets spiritual growth, and this is true of the pastor to the seminary student, the stay-at-home mom to the teenager, and beyond.

So how do we endure? How do we remain faithful day in and day out and consistently engage in the spiritual disciplines? We abide in Him. We live out of our identities as children of God. We keep our eyes fixed on Christ, who is the "source and perfecter of our faith" (Hebrews 12:2). Like Him, we endure with the joy of our future glorification set before us. We keep an eternal perspective. We refuse to grow weary or give up.

And we do all of this with the indwelling Spirit, and through the Spirit, we experience His fruit. We experience and exhibit love, joy, peace, patience, kindness, goodness, faithfulness, gentleness, and self-control (Galatians 5:22-23). This is the fruit of a life committed to doing the hard work of everyday faithfulness. This work may last a lifetime, but we remain steadfast with the hope that the glory and fruit will last for all eternity.

Abide in Him.

READ MATTHEW 11:28-30. HOW DOES THE PICTURE OF THE YOKE HELP YOU UNDERSTAND THE CHRISTIAN LIFE?

READ EPHESIANS 2:8-9. HOW DO FAITH AND GOOD WORKS CO-EXIST IN THE CHRISTIAN LIFE?

HOW DOES LOOKING TO JESUS HELP US RUN OUR RACE OF FAITH WITH ENDURANCE? HOW WOULD THIS LOOK PRACTICALLY IN YOUR EVERYDAY LIFE?

WEEK 4 MEMORY VERSE

Trust in Him at all times, you people; pour out your hearts before him. God is our refuge. Selah.

—

PSALM 62:8

Week Four Reflection
REVIEW ALL PASSAGES FROM THE WEEK

SUMMARIZE THE MAIN PRINCIPLES YOU LEARNED.

WHAT DID YOU OBSERVE ABOUT GOD'S CHARACTER?

WHAT DID YOU LEARN ABOUT THE CONDITION OF MANKIND AND ABOUT YOURSELF?

HOW WERE YOU POINTED TO THE GOSPEL?

HOW DOES THE GOSPEL ENCOURAGE AND EMPOWER YOU TO PURSUE GODLINESS, AND WHAT SPECIFIC ACTION STEPS CAN YOU TAKE TO IMPLEMENT THE SPIRITUAL DISCIPLINES COVERED THIS WEEK?

WRITE A PRAYER RESPONDING TO WHAT YOU HAVE STUDIED THIS WEEK. ADORE GOD FOR HIS CHARACTER. CONFESS THE SIN THAT HE HAS REVEALED IN YOUR OWN LIFE THIS WEEK. PRAY FOR THOSE WHO THE LORD BROUGHT TO MIND AS YOU STUDIED THIS WEEK.

WHAT IS *the gospel?*

THANK YOU FOR READING AND ENJOYING THIS STUDY WITH US! WE ARE ABUNDANTLY GRATEFUL FOR THE WORD OF GOD, THE INSTRUCTION WE GLEAN FROM IT, AND THE EVER-GROWING UNDERSTANDING ABOUT GOD'S CHARACTER FROM IT. WE ARE ALSO THANKFUL THAT SCRIPTURE CONTINUALLY POINTS TO ONE THING IN INNUMERABLE WAYS: THE GOSPEL.

We remember our brokenness when we read about the fall of Adam and Eve in the garden of Eden (Genesis 3), when sin entered into a perfect world and maimed it. We remember the necessity that something innocent must die to pay for our sin when we read about the atoning sacrifices in the Old Testament. We read that we have all sinned and fallen short of the glory of God (Romans 3:23) and that the penalty for our brokenness, the wages of our sin, is death (Romans 6:23). We all are in need of grace and mercy, but most importantly, we all need a Savior.

We consider the goodness of God when we realize that He did not plan to leave us in this dire state. We see His promise to buy us back from the clutches of sin and death in Genesis 3:15. And we see that promise accomplished with Jesus Christ on the cross. Jesus Christ knew no sin yet became sin so that we might become righteous through His sacrifice (2 Corinthians 5:21). Jesus was tempted in every way that we are and lived sinlessly. He was reviled yet still yielded Himself for our sake, that we may have life abundant in Him. Jesus lived the perfect life that we could not live and died the death that we deserved.

The gospel is profound yet simple. There are many mysteries in it that we can never exhaust this side of heaven, but there is still overwhelming weight to its implications in this life. The gospel is the telling of our sinfulness and God's goodness, and this gracious gift compels a response. We are saved by grace through faith, which means

that we rest with faith in the grace that Jesus Christ displayed on the cross (Ephesians 2:8-9). We cannot save ourselves from our brokenness or do any amount of good works to merit God's favor, but we can have faith that what Jesus accomplished in His death, burial, and resurrection was more than enough for our salvation and our eternal delight. When we accept God, we are commanded to die to our self and our sinful desires and live a life worthy of the calling we have received (Ephesians 4:1). The gospel compels us to be sanctified, and in so doing, we are conformed to the likeness of Christ Himself. This is hope. This is redemption. This is the gospel.

SCRIPTURE TO REFERENCE:

GENESIS 3:15	*I will put hostility between you and the woman, and between your offspring and her offspring. He will strike your head, and you will strike his heel.*
ROMANS 3:23	*For all have sinned and fall short of the glory of God.*
ROMANS 6:23	*For the wages of sin is death, but the gift of God is eternal life in Christ Jesus our Lord.*
2 CORINTHIANS 5:21	*He made the one who did not know sin to be sin for us, so that in him we might become the righteousness of God.*
EPHESIANS 2:8-9	*For you are saved by grace through faith, and this is not from yourselves; it is God's gift—not from works, so that no one can boast.*
EPHESIANS 4:1	*Therefore I, the prisoner in the Lord, urge you to walk worthy of the calling you have received,*

*Thank you for studying
God's Word with us!*

CONNECT WITH US

@thedailygraceco

@kristinschmucker

CONTACT US

info@thedailygraceco.com

SHARE

#thedailygraceco

#lampandlight

VISIT US ONLINE

thedailygraceco.com

MORE DAILY GRACE

The Daily Grace App

Daily Grace Podcast